JESUS, OUR BURDEN BEARER

By Josephine Fitzgerald

ROYALTY PUBLISHING COMPANY
P.O. Box 2125
Bedford, IN 47421

Copyright © 2001 by Josephine Fitzgerald
All rights reserved.

Royalty Publishing Company
P.O. Box 2125
Bedford, IN 47421

ISBN 0-910487-49-9
Library of Congress Catalog Number: Requested

DEDICATION
To Jesus
My Savior and Lord

ACKNOWLEDGMENTS

I thank all the many people who have helped work on this book and helped bring it to completion: to those who have given their testimonies; to the board members: Carol Megginson, David Swing, Betty & Emmett Dunnevant for direction and advice; to Olga Skorackyj and Faye Bailey who have once again done the editing and typing; to all who have helped get the books distributed; and a special thank you to Nita Scoggan who has worked with me to prepare my books for publication. I love each of you.

Other books by Josephine Fitzgerald

**WHEN THOU PASSEST THROUGH THE WATERS
PRECIOUS MEMORIES
I FOUND THE ANSWER...I PRAYED
WE GROW IN THE VALLEYS**

No books are sold.
If you wish to help with the cost of production, you may send to:
**Josephine Fitzgerald
112 Anderson Lane
Lovingston, VA 22949**

No one will be refused a book if they cannot afford to give.

FOREWORD

I received a nice letter from Dr. Henry the other day. At the close he wrote, "If you have another book in you, the Lord will provide the time to write it." As I read that, I thought, "I do not feel the least bit inclined to write another book." Then came along a letter from Sylvia. She had a song sheet in it, and that triggered this book. The song is as follows:

WHEN JESUS TOOK MY BURDEN

Verse I
When I a poor, lost sinner, Before the Lord did fall,
And in the name of Jesus For pardon loud did call;
He heard my supplication, And soon the weak was strong,
For Jesus took my burden, And left me with a song.

Verse II
Oft-time the way is dreary, And rugged seems the road,
Oft-times I'm weak and weary, When bent beneath some load;
But when I cry in weakness, "How long, O Lord, how long?"
Then Jesus takes my burden, And leaves me with a song.

Verse III
When I was crushed with sorrow I bowed in deep despair,
My load of grief and heart-ache Seemed more than I could bear;
'Twas then I heard a whisper, "You to the Lord belong."
Then Jesus took my burden, And left me with a song.

Verse IV
I'll trust Him for the future, He knoweth all the way,
For with His eyes He'll guide me Along life's pilgrim way;
And I will tell in heaven, While ages roll along,
How Jesus took my burden and left me with a song.

Chorus
Yes, Jesus took my burden I could no longer bear,
Yes Jesus took my burden In answer to my prayer;
My anxious fears subsided my spirit was made strong,
For Jesus took my burden, And left me with a song.

Johnson Oatman, Jr.

PREFACE

As I sit here at my desk, being captivated by the silence of the study where I often retreat, my mind travels seeking to gather the thoughts worthy of an introduction to the volume before you. So much can be said at the outset of a selected reading, however, in this volume are contained a significant plethora of thoughts expressed in words that are testimony of the hearts of those who convey them. A preface that is fitting, then, might be sufficient in one further witness, which would be, my own.

This is the fifth volume in a series of testimonies written by one whose life is an inspiration to many, including me. Mrs. Mary Fitzgerald, "Josephine" as we call her, is one who I am privileged to know. She started out as my Sunday School teacher and then, subsequently, I became her pastor. So very few there are who can be looked upon as rendering a genuinely humble Christian example. Josephine is one of these. I am honored and grateful indeed to be asked to introduce this text for her.

The word "testimony", (Gk. "marturia"), means witness or perhaps evidence. Evidence then, in this context, would be derived from the expression of a converted heart or soul. One who is given, by the sovereign grace of God, life where there is no life, has flowing from their regenerated heart the ability to believe and to show outwardly the testimony of this divine transposition. Therefore, what is presented before you in the following pages is simply the witness or evidence of those individuals who desire to share with other believers, as well as to those who are lost, their evidence of truth which resides in them. Further, the simple act of faith, which is also a gift of God enabling us to believe, is the only means to receive The One Who is the focus of this blessed redeeming grace. This One is The Eternal God, Who is The Living Lord Jesus Christ.

Isaac Watts once wrote in his great hymn, "At the Cross", that it was there that the "...burden of my heart rolled away...". When one is redeemed in Christ's precious shed blood, which at Calvary was shed as a payment for the sins of every believer, this burden is taken from the believer and placed upon Him. Christ Who knew no sin was made sin for us that, in turn, we might have imputed to us His righteousness. The first declaration of God, regarding Christ becoming our propitiation, was not our salvation but rather the declaration of Christ's righteousness (Rom. 3:25-26). Because of Christ's perfect righteousness, He was able to render to God what we could never repay, the payment for the penalty of our sin. Therefore, in Paul's writing of this divine declaration, God can declare "just" those who are not so. We have then, as believers, imputed to us Christ's righteousness while our sin is imputed to Him. The sobering reality that we should see is that Christ is devoid of all sin and could not possibly have sin in Him, so we are devoid of all righteousness and can have none in ourselves. This divine condescension is the miracle of God's salvation for us.

Christ, alone, sustains us and will do so throughout eternity (1 Thess. 5:23-24). At no time in the ages to come will we be able to stand independent of Christ's perfect righteousness being imputed to us. Christ, my friend, is the sole bearer of the believer's guilt and sin, having washed it away in His shed blood. He died on the cross and was "bodily" raised again from the grave so that we may have eternal life with Him.

Truly, in the thoughts expressed by Isaac Watts in his testimony, it is at the cross where we see the light and the "burden" of our heart is rolled away. Because of this dreadful burden of sin that we inherited from Adam, who was the federal head of the human race, we truly have no hope in ourselves. Yet, here is the good news of the Gospel, that God in His infinite mercy has received full payment for this debt in the perfect redemptive work of Christ, so that this burden is lifted by faith in Jesus Christ. We may, in spite of the world around us with all of its woes, be "...happy all the day...". This happiness is in the blessed hope of our eternal redemption.

Christ has lifted the burden of sin for every believer. He is also the One Who carries us onward through each consecutive moment of life that He gives to us. As we traverse this trail of tears and look forward to that day when we shall see Him face to face beholding the "beatific vision", we can rest assured that He will carry our burdens now, just as certain as we will be shed of them forever in glory.

Perhaps the greatest mark of Christian maturity is the surrendering, with complete trust, our cares and concerns of this pilgrimage of our Lord. He takes care of His sheep and He knows them (John 10: 27-30). He keeps us from falling (Jude 1, 24). We know that all things work together for good to those whom He has called (Rom. 8:28-30). To walk with Him in His will and to be in tune with the leading of His Holy Spirit brings such a peace, which certainly does pass all understanding. Truly, He sustains His own. Their burdens become light and, certainly, the hope of every child of God far transcends the affairs and concerns of this brief passage.

As you read the witness of those in this volume, my prayer and certainly the prayer of its author, Josephine, is that you also may know this One Who is willing to give you life, to give you His righteousness, and to take away the burden of your sin.

The apostle Peter in his witness to the Sanhedrin declared in clear concise terms, *"Neither is there salvation in any other; for there is no other name under Heaven given among men, whereby we must be saved." (Acts 4:12).* This volume is the witness of this magnificent name and Person. May your hearts be blessed and may your burden be lifted as you surrender all to the only bearer, The Living Lord Jesus Christ.

In Christ,
Rev. David R. Swing

TABLE OF CONTENTS

Dedication & Acknowledgment..	II
Foreword...	III
Song - WHEN JESUS TOOK MY BURDEN.................	IV
Preface...	V

PART I

CHAPTERS	PAGES
1-Our Lord Has Lovely Surprises Along the Way........	9
2-Our Lord Has a Reason for All Things.....................	12
3-Studying the Bible..	14
4-Stephanie's High Graduation..................................	16
5-A Lovely Vacation on the Coan River......................	17
6-A Great Warrior Has Gone Home...........................	21
7-Remembering the Past..	24
8-Testimonies of Others...	27
9-Another Wonderful Answer to Prayer......................	49
10-Good News about Pat Mendoza............................	51
11-Times Flies...	55
12-Our Lord Feeds His Own......................................	57
13-Changes All Around...	59
14-An Unexpected Birthday Party..............................	61
15-All Creatures Great and Small..............................	63
16-Angie's Graduation from Nursing School..............	65
17-Sitting Under the Word...	67
18-Stick to the Word of God......................................	68
19-The Lord Has Implanted the Holy Spirit in Each Person as They Are Born Again...............	70
20-Vacation Bible School - 1985................................	72
21-Good to Get Home..	79
22-The Miracle Lady..	81
PART II -Testimony of Heang Oak Horn......................	83
PART III-A Ten Year History of Immanuel Baptist Church, Richmond, Virginia....................	127

Chapter One

OUR LORD HAS LOVELY SURPRISES ALONG THE WAY

Ephesians 3:20 Now unto him that is able to do exceeding abundantly above all that we ask or think, according to the power that worketh in us,

My book, **We Grow in the Valleys** came out just before Christmas,1998, which was an answer to prayer, as I could share them with my loved ones along with their gifts. The day after Christmas, Angie, my granddaughter, and her two friends, Joe and Monica, came from Florida and stayed until January 2nd. While here they lived on the ski slopes of Wintergreen, which is about fifteen miles from my home. Joe had not seen snow since he was a little boy but he took to it like a duck takes to water. Joe is very special to Angie; they are talking about marriage. While at my home we talked a lot about the Lord and Joe captured my heart.

Angie's sister, Nicole, came with her friend, Mark, and they stayed with their mother, Brenda, in Charlottesville. While all were here, Brenda brought her food to my home and we all ate together. Nicole brought a couple of her friends over also. We all enjoyed ourselves very much.

On the 2nd of January, when they started back, they talked me into going back with them. Angie packed the car the night before we left. She put my suitcase and a box of her clothes on top of the car with those cords you use to hold luggage. We left early the next morning. The weatherman was predicting an ice storm and we wanted to miss it. From my house to I-64 we had to stop three or four times, as my suitcase and her box of clothes slid off the roof and landed right in the middle of the road! Angie would have to turn back and get out of the car and dart between traffic to get my suitcase and pick up her clothes all over the road. After about the third or forth time of trying to fix them she somehow managed to put them on the inside of the trunk. They had a full load coming and had bought several things to take home for souvenirs, so it was a miracle they could fit mine in. We drove as far as St. Matthews, S.C. Ashley, my great-grandson, and his family live there. He and his wife, Tammy, had just had a little baby, so I got to see my great-great-granddaughter. She is so cute; they named her Presley. I call her Precious.

Ashley's mother, Connie, had a cabin right next to Ashley's place, so we put our things in her cabin, and we all went down to her main house to see her. Her husband, Jack, was sick, and I believe I took what he had while I was there. Shortly after I got to my son Tommy's house, I came down sick. I was on the phone with my doctor so much, I was wishing I had brought him with me. I know that would have worked out fine, don't you?

After I got over being sick, I had a wonderful time. Tommy, Angie, Joe and I all went on a cruise. We saw many beautiful homes owned by millionaires. The captain told us how they made their money.

On that cruise, I made friends with some wonderful people from New Jersey. She gave me a picture of her husband in his Scottish kilts with his bagpipes.

Joe's family lives in Sunrise, Florida. He has a wonderful family. Jeanette, his mother, took Angie and I to a lovely Tea Room for lunch one day. Another friend, Alicia, took me to a restaurant called Ruby-Tuesdays. Afterward she took me shopping and bought me two of those little animals that are all the rage now. Evelyn Rogers lives two doors down from us. We visited each other quite a bit. When I left, she brought me a lovely soap dish in the form of a seashell.

My son, Bobby, came down while I was there. We all had a wonderful time together. Tommy had off the whole six weeks that I was there. He was called back to work the day I left. The Lord opened many doors to witness for Him.

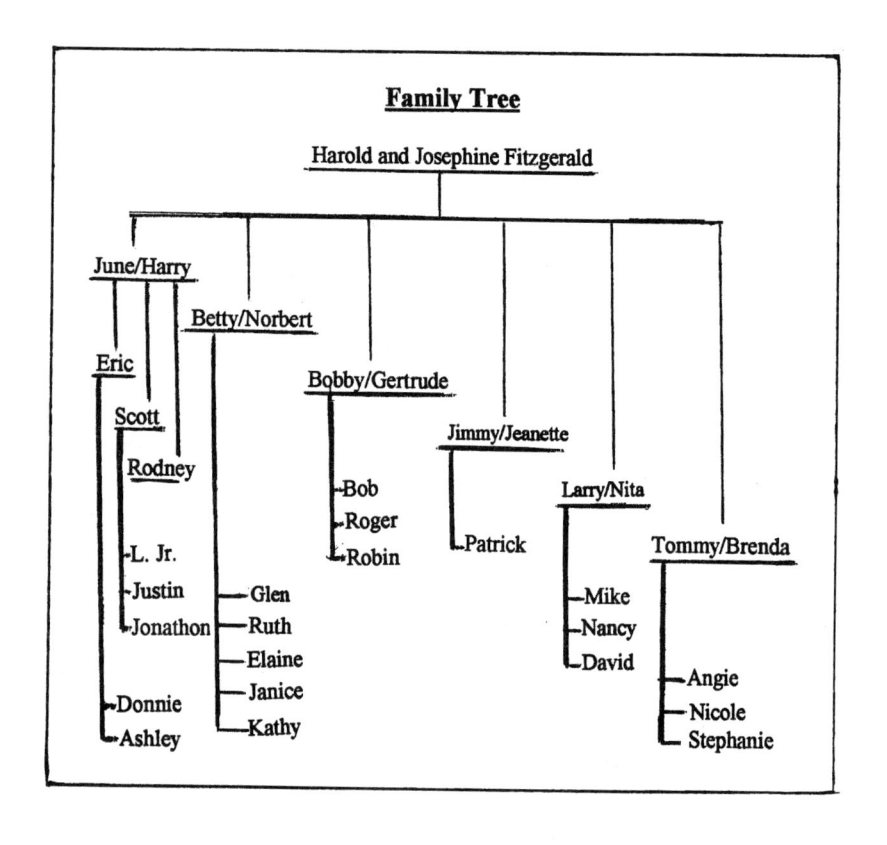

Family Tree

Harold and Josephine Fitzgerald

- **June/Harry**
  - Eric
    - L. Jr.
    - Justin
    - Jonathon
  - Scott
  - Rodney
  - Donnie
  - Ashley
- **Betty/Norbert**
  - Glen
  - Ruth
  - Elaine
  - Janice
  - Kathy
- **Bobby/Gertrude**
  - Bob
  - Roger
  - Robin
- **Jimmy/Jeanette**
  - Patrick
- **Larry/Nita**
  - Mike
  - Nancy
  - David
- **Tommy/Brenda**
  - Angie
  - Nicole
  - Stephanie

♥ I do want to thank the Lord for all of my wonderful family. They are a blessing to me.

Chapter Two

OUR LORD HAS A REASON FOR ALL THINGS

Philippians 4:13   I can do all things through Christ which strengtheneth me.

After staying six weeks with Tommy, he, Bobby and Nicole drove me to Ft. Myers, Florida to my nephew's home. While at his home we had the joy of picking grapefruit from a tree. We stayed a few days. When we got there, Betty-Jo, my daughter, and her husband, Norbert, and daughter Elaine, came to pick me up and take me to visit in their home in Alabama.

I stayed six weeks with them. Betty Jo always puts herself out to take me to see many things, especially to look at mobile homes. She wants me to sell my home in Virginia and get a mobile home and move there where she can look after me. I always remind her that when she was looking after my brother, Anthony, I had gall-bladder surgery. When I got out of the hospital, I had to come home and look after myself. The Lord was there and I got along fine. The Lord looks after His own. When I needed help, someone would come by with food or just to visit.

After six weeks they brought me home in time for the Easter cantata at my church. It was one of the best ones that I have been privileged to hear.

When we got back we found out that my grandson, Eric, was planning on moving in with me.   He has prostate cancer and the doctors don't give him over two years to live. He had surgery, but they failed to get it all, although he is now in remission. Eric is older than Tommy, so he seems more like a son than a grandson. All his people have gone on except one younger brother.

When we really want the Lord's will in our lives, He won't let us make a mistake. One other time I was sure that I was to sell and move. He again held me back from making a mistake. Now again, He has shown me not to sell. Betty-Jo and Norbert have told me, when I can't handle the situation, they would come down and help me with Eric. Betty-Jo and Norbert both have servants' hearts. Wherever there is a need, they pick up and go help that person.

This past Sunday was Mother's day. Bobby, his friend, Mildred, and her mother all came down on Saturday, and Bobby took us to a lovely restaurant called Country Cooking. They have very good food. I am afraid I am being spoiled, and I sort of like it. The Wednesday before, Faye and Olga took me to the Golden Corral for lunch. If you remember, they are the two who edited and prepared my book for the printer.

Sunday at church, I got a lovely corsage. I was the oldest mother there. I was ninety the January before. It is hard to realize I am that old. Yes, I am having physical problems, hard of hearing, trouble with my eyes and still limp some from my broken hip. But, oh, the joy in my heart. As I go about my work there is always a hymn going through my mind, even when I awake during the night a song is there.

I still teach Sunday School, although I find out for all my studying, I still have to lean hard on the Lord. Only He knows what the ones in my class need. I do not want to teach a lesson, but to say something that will meet their need.

Chapter Three

STUDYING THE BIBLE

2 Timothy 2:15 Study to shew thyself approved unto God, a workman that needeth not to be ashamed, rightly dividing the word of truth.

David Swing came to our church as our pastor in September a year ago. He knows the scriptures, and is always studying. He and his wife, Vikki, have a thirteen year old daughter, Margaret and a sixteen year old son, Jorge, who lives with his grandmother in Lynchburg, so he can graduate with his class. Vikki and David are in my Sunday School class. I enjoy sitting under his preaching and in Bible class on Sunday nights. I also went on Wednesday nights, until I left in January to visit my son in Florida. When I got back on Easter Sunday, they turned the class back to me. Anna Harris taught it while I was gone.

This coming Sunday our lesson will be from the book of Genesis. There is so much in that first chapter, especially the first two verses.

We know when God created the heavens and the earth, it was complete. Yet, the second verse shows us an entirely different picture. Showing us that between the first and second verse, there was some kind of judgment. Everything was wrapped up in total darkness. We see the HOLY SPIRIT hovering over it. One day the Lord called out, *"Let there be light"*, and the light appeared. The light was already there, but the dark was so intense that it didn't show through. Things that were already there began to appear, first light from darkness, then night and day. Second, waters from the waters, rain clouds up in the sky separated and waters below; lakes, rivers and oceans were formed. When the light hit the ground the vegetables and the fruit began to appear. It only needed the warmth of the sun to bring it forth, each after its own kind.

The second creative act was the creation of the animal. The third creative act was when God made man from the dust of the ground and breathed into his nostrils the breath of life. We notice it was the Trinity that created man; Father, Son and the Holy Ghost. In Genesis 1:26 we read, *"And God said, Let us make man in our image, after our likeness:"* Eve was created in Adam. God caused a deep sleep to fall upon Adam and took a rib out of his side and formed Eve. I heard a doctor say, that was the first c-section performed.

Chapter Four

STEPHANIE'S HIGH SCHOOL GRADUATION

Psalm 32:8 I will instruct thee and teach thee in the way which thou shalt go: I will guide thee with mine eye.

Stephanie was the vice-president of her class and oh, what a day, when we all went to the graduation. While Bobby was allowed to take the car closer to the bleachers because of my health, I still had a long way to walk. I barely made it. When I approached the stand I said, "I have to sit down." The bleachers were filled, but a lovely black lady got up and gave me her seat, and held her umbrella over me to keep the sun off. The others had to go to the top of the bleachers. Bobby sent Nicole down to tell me to stay seated; he would bring the car all the way down to get me.

After it was over we went back to Stephanie's house for fellowship and food. Her mother, Brenda, had brought so much food that Phillip, a friend of Brenda's, stayed outside cooking a large ham, roast beef, hot dogs and hamburgers. Later, Bobby took me home. Chris and Eric came over and put in my air-conditioner. The Lord is so good, letting everything fall into place. Eric, fifty-two, is my oldest grandchild and Stephanie, who is seventeen, is my youngest grandchild.

Chapter Five

A LOVELY VACATION ON THE COAN RIVER

1 Timothy 6:17 ... the living God, who giveth us richly all things to enjoy;

About a week ago, we came up to the Coan River. We first went by Bobby's home in Richmond to pick up the key and get the materials that Eric would need to paint the inside of Bobby's house. We also got the key to Roger's place for me to stay while Eric did the painting. They each have a beautiful home there. My late husband, Harold, and Bobby discovered the land all grown up in weeds. They both built small cabins on the land. Mark also bought some land there which he later sold to Bobby. Harold sold our place to Tommy, who later sold it to Bobby and now Bobby's three children have lovely homes on the property. Bobby's daughter has the largest one, Bobby's is second largest, but Roger's is the one where I generally go to stay. He has many skylights in the place. It has three bedrooms, two bathrooms and a large living room, which opens to the dinning and kitchen area. The grandchildren are precious to me. They will give me the keys to their homes, and let me bring my friends there.

While Eric is painting the inside of Bob's home, I am vacationing at Roger's place.

Betty and Emmett Dunnevant came down that Friday and we had a wonderful time. They brought a full meal for all of us. They, too, have servants' hearts, always doing for others. One of the neighbors came Saturday to visit me. Sunday, Mrs. Hundley came and took me to church; it was homecoming and we had a delightful time. She picked me up for Women's Missionary Union meeting the following night. I was getting pretty lonesome as Eric is mostly in the other house painting. Every once in a while he comes over to check on me. As he comes in the door he sings out, "Honey, I'm home." He thinks because I am ninety years old, I shouldn't do anything, so he wants to cook the meals. I have to admit, he is a good cook. In a way, I feel ashamed, as he is working hard over there. He loves to tease me and say he does the cooking so he won't have to eat mine.

All the children and grandchildren think at ninety I have done my part. I'm afraid I love the spoiling and that is not good. I want my life to count for the Lord. The greatest desire of my heart is to live as close to my Lord as a sinner saved by grace can.

While enjoying it here, I do miss my church. I have enjoyed the churches I have visited, but to me, my church is the best. David Swing is a unique preacher. I pray that he will not try so hard to please everyone, that he will just turn it all over to the Lord, and go in the strength of the Lord. We can't do it alone, but we can <u>let Christ work through us.</u>

I had a delightful phone call this morning from Ruth Fisher. She was in my Sunday School class years ago. I am looking forward to seeing her again. She plans on coming down sometime this week. Everybody in this area is asking for my books.

God opened up a way to put the books in the State Fair. Betty Dunnevant's son-in-law, Billy, manages the State Fair in Richmond, Virginia. She approached him and he said the booths are around five hundred dollars each. We knew that was out, since we didn't have that kind of money, but Billy couldn't get it off his mind. The Southern Baptist Convention had two booths, so Billy approached them about the books. They let us share a booth, and I believe about twelve hundred books were given out. Our Lord is wonderful. When I hear how the Lord has used the books to help various people, I praise and thank Him. I remember how He had to let me be in a car wreck, lying upside down for fourteen hours before I was found. Over and over He gave me the verse Romans 8:28, in order to get my attention. He wanted me to write a book. Even then I argued with Him, telling Him that I never had the education to do it. But once I yielded to Him, how the memories began to flow. The writing of the first book wasn't hard, as He flooded my memory with what had happened. Living through it was the hardest. I praise the Lord, if I hadn't gone through what I did, I would never come to know my Lord in such a precious way. The Lord sent a Spirit-filled lady into my life. She is the one that led me into a deep walk with Him. May the Lord ever send people to me that I can lead to a deeper walk with Him. The time down here has turned into a beautiful vacation. It is quiet here; you can feel the presence of the Lord. My desire is to one day invite quite a few of my friends and have a Prayer Seminar here. How wonderful that would be if Dr. Henry would come to this area and hold one. Then maybe the churches would begin to ask him to their churches. It will take many prayers to bring it to pass.

    In another hour, Eric is taking me to the health center to get my flu shot. I'll be glad to get that behind me.

    I think I mentioned to you about Eric having prostate cancer; he also has a disk in his back that goes out from time to time and hinders him from painting. We have talked it over and when we get back, he has to go to Washington, D.C. and get some things straightened out, then to John Hopkins Hospital to be checked out. He is coming back to my house and check into UVA and have the back surgery.

    Today my heart is mostly on Norbert, my son-in-law. He is having heart surgery. That man has suffered so much. He was shell-shocked in World War II and when he hears a sudden noise, he goes all to pieces. We can all be sitting around the table and a pain will strike him, it will last for quite a few minutes, then it will let up.

Won't it be wonderful when the Lord comes back and takes us to be with Him, no more sorrow, no more pain? How wonderful most of all, when we will see Him face to face. I think of that hymn, "Face to Face with Christ my Savior".

I was thinking about being here and longing to go back home, not appreciating the wonderful vacation our Lord had planned for me. Back in the days when I would go on my back porch and ask the Lord if there was anything out there that I could gather and cook for our dinner. I was from the city and my husband had been raised on a farm. I know in the books I write I often repeat myself. I marvel at how much patience the Lord has with me. Some lessons He has to teach me over and over until it was there to stay. Many times I let Him down, but <u>He has never let me down</u>. He sees into my heart the desire and the longing to be open to Him, that He may be able to work through me. Over and over I marvel that He chose me before the foundation of the earth. Thank you Lord so very much.

Chapter Six

A GREAT WARRIOR HAS GONE HOME

2 Timothy 4:7 I have fought a good fight, I have finished my course, I have kept the faith:

Eric had come in to fix supper and we were there playing little game while eating. The phone rang and it was Norbert. He and Eric talked for quite a while, teasing each other about Norbert getting a pig's valve to his heart. The next day was beautiful and everything seemed to be in order. I was looking forward to seeing Ruth Fisher. She had called that she was coming. I heard a car drive up, and expecting Ruth, I went to the door. It was my son, Bobby, and his friend, Mildred. I was glad to see them. He told me that Betty-Jo had called and told them that Norbert had gone to be with the Lord. Eric and I were shocked to hear the news. I quickly got my things together and we started back to Richmond, where Bobby lives. When we arrived at his house, Stephanie called from Lovingston, to ask him if he would wait for her; she wanted to go with us to Alabama. We left the next morning and arrived in plenty of time for the funeral. Bobby and Stephanie went home right after the funeral, but I stayed a month with Betty-Jo.

We were all praying that he would come through the surgery. For years they knew that he needed it. The operation went fine, but they couldn't stop the bleeding and he died. They tried to get the blood to clot, but failed. I think it was just the Lord's time to take him home to be with Him. Betty-Jo had always prayed that the Lord would take him first, as she felt he couldn't make it without her. However, she wasn't expecting it at this point. He was 76 years old.

Betty-Jo and Norbert had always worked together, except for a short time when he worked for the Gas and Electric Company. Their work was mostly in Christian Schools. He was a principal and teacher and she and her daughter, Elaine, were teachers.

Norbert was a man that loved to witness for his Lord. For years he would go to Hardee's and have his breakfast. Always a double order of sausage and gravy biscuits, talking to everyone he met about his Lord. One day when I was visiting with them, we all went to Wal-Mart to get some things. We had no sooner gotten through the door, when several people came to him to talk. One was a professor in college, which wanted him to come to speak to his class. He tutored people just to get in a word about the Lord. His whole life was lived for Christ. He was human just like all of us and would at times lose his temper. He always humbled himself and would go back and ask for forgiveness. When he did something that he didn't think was right, he would get on his knees and cry out to the Lord for forgiveness. He and Betty-Jo had many people work against them and lie about them. He never held it against them. If he could, he would go out of his way to be nice to them.

To get back to the funeral, never have I seen so much food brought into a home. Two churches, many neighbors, and people as far away as 30 miles were bringing it. His people from Wisconsin and many on our side were there and yet we didn't make a dent in the food. Betty-Jo's freezer was filled and she carried several boxes of food to a family with five children. What a testimony to the unsaved as to how the Lord provides for His own.

The funeral was held on Monday. Bobby and Pat, my grandson, were pallbearers. There were three preachers on the platform; a former pastor, his present pastor and a pastor from the home church of two of his daughters who live in Florida. The former pastor, Rev. Bobby Carpenter spoke first. With tears in his eyes he began to tell about his experiences with Norbert. He started by saying, "The last time I was down here to preach a revival, Norbert and I started talking after the service; people began to leave and we were still talking. They turned the lights out, and we were still talking. We stayed in the dark, still talking." He said the Lord spoke to him and said, "You better listen to this man, you may not get another chance to hear him."

Then Norbert's pastor, John Bush spoke. He, too, had tears in his eyes as he told how Norbert would always encourage him to stand firm. When it seemed so many were against him, the Lord would see him through.

The third pastor from Florida told when Norbert and Betty Jo would come to visit their daughters, Norbert would attend their church and always encourage him.

Norbert's pastor said, "There is no such thing as a short service for Norbert, there was to much to tell. We are not exalting Norbert, but telling how he exalted his Lord."

Betty-Jo had perfect peace about his going. She said, "I could not wish him back. He is where he always wanted to be."

No matter what people said about him, they always had to say, "He was good to his family."

Chapter Seven

REMEMBERING THE PAST

Psalm 34:7 The angel of the LORD encampeth round about them that fear him, and delivereth them.

Back during World War II we were living in a lovely home, the nicest one I had ever lived in. Rents were soaring, but the landlady had not raised our rent because the government put rent control into effect. When it dawned on her that she couldn't raise our rent, she put the house up for sale. They had to give us six months to get out. Houses were hard to find. We looked everywhere and finally one day, Harold, my husband came across this old house that was just a shell. The roof leaked something terrible. The night he came home and told us he had found a place and did I want to go and look at it, I was quite excited. When we got there and I first saw it, my heart sank within me. I couldn't believe he was taking me to live in that old place.

He went the next day and put a down payment on the place. He began to take the two boys that were in high school, out, and on his way to work would drop them off at the house and put them to work on the place. He would come back at noon and check on them. After work he went back and they all worked till dark. It was about the fifteenth of February and time for us to move. They had only been able to get the pantry and kitchen fixed enough so that we could have heat. We had to put large heavy curtains over the remaining doorways. The weather was beautiful the day we moved so I was much encouraged thinking that spring had come early. Two days later we had the worse snowstorm of the winter. Everything had stopped and we had to dig in the snow to get firewood to keep warm. The bad weather lasted for about six weeks before it started to get warmer.

As our place was two hundred feet off the main road we all had to get behind the car and push while Harold tried to get it started. We had no electric lights, an outdoor toilet that was about to cave in, kerosene lamps, and a well that went dry. We often had to carry our water from a neighbor that lived about one half mile from us. Those were hectic days for me, as I had always lived in the city and had all the conveniences, but my husband was raised in the country and had been used to many of those things. I know if I hadn't known my Lord I would not have been able to make it. He was so real to me at that time. Truly He had His angels watching over me. There is no other answer. Those were the days that helped me to draw closer to Him. He can give you peace regardless of what you are faced with, if you keep your eyes on Him.

When I became pregnant, Harold realized it would be hard to take care of a baby at night without lights, so he had a friend come and wire our house. How wonderful to have lights again. Shortly after that he lost his business. It would have been easier if he had been a Christian, but he had refused to open his heart to the Lord and was very rebellious.

We had very little food. I remember walking to the door and looking out and asking the Lord if there was anything out there that I could cook. One night I remember standing at my ironing board, talking to the Lord and calling out to the Him for food. All we had in the house was a box of cornflakes but no milk or sugar. I told the Lord that the children needed food and would He please send us some, and then I said, "Lord, even if you sent it I am so tired I don't think I could cook it." The Lord heard my prayer and sent one of His angels to nudge my neighbor and lay it on her heart to come over and offer ice cream and cake. She wanted me to come to her house and eat it. At first I told her I was too tired. The Lord spoke to me and told me to go. So we gathered up the children and went across the yard to her house. As we went in the door, her table was just like she had left it when they finished their supper. She looked at me and asked me if we had eaten yet. I told her no, so she had us sit down and eat supper since she and her husband didn't like leftovers. There was ham, green beans, sliced tomatoes, potatoes and tall glasses of ice tea. Then after supper she served the ice cream and cake. I went home a new person that night and with a deeper faith in my Lord. Even to this day when I go to bed I ask the Lord to send His angels to protect me so I can go to sleep. I am 91 now, and am never afraid, as I know the Lord is here and will keep me from all harm.

On another occasion, when I was a new Christian, Harold had gone to Florida to take a new job. They had to train him and gave him very little pay, so he hadn't been able to send me any money. The Lord supplied all our needs and some of our wants at this time. *Philippians 4:19 But my God shall supply all your need according to his riches in glory by Christ Jesus.*

Chapter Eight

TESTIMONIES OF OTHERS

This is a chapter of testimonies and letters I have received from various people.

TESTIMONY OF JANE PHIPPS

Josephine,

Received your wonderful letter today. I am always so glad to hear from you. Our Lord is so good. He surely is my very best friend. I knew He would supply my needs. He sure has taken very good care of me for the past two years. It seems like every day I grow closer and stronger in my wonderful Savior. I received one of my Bible studies back, and a note from the lady that grades them. She is a dear person. She said that I was an excellent student. That's because learning more and more about my Lord is my heart's desire. I want to learn more and more about my wonderful Lord. I love to study my Bible, and it amazes me when I see something that I've read and overlooked. God's word is powerful.

I was thinking yesterday about my life two years ago. The day the judge gave me five years. I never thought I could ever make it. Isn't our Lord wonderful? Look at me now! I have more peace and joy in my heart than I ever thought possible and I'm in prison. God is so wonderful, Josephine. He has brought me so far. I thank God there were people out there praying for me. I sure wasn't. I wouldn't even acknowledge God's Word.

I know that God is with me and He won't put more on me than I can bear. I know I am a child of God and I'm not afraid of things like I used to be. I know the devil wants me to worry and fear and I'm not!

Here I sit in a prison cell,
I have a story I need to tell.
For stupid crimes I've come to prison,
Lord, those Xanax's took all my reason.
I thought they were giving me a helping hand,
But they took my floor, I couldn't stand.
Because of my crimes, all my rights I lost,
Losing my children, my family, what a cost.

I'll tell you a secret, I'll tell you no lie,
Don't use pills for a crutch, I'll tell you why.
I thought this is medicine, I'm not on drugs,
But Lord look I've lost some precious hugs.
I lived for those pills in a bottle or bag,
Walking around like a crazy old hag.
I remember a time when I thought I was bad,
Just look at me now, I've lost everything I had.

I took lots of pride in myself, especially my hair,
But one day I found I no longer cared.
I used to have a lot of gold,
But most was taken, some I sold.
I seemed to hurt all who crossed my path,
Some days I didn't even take a bath.
My hair even has fallen out,
My appearance became ugly without a doubt.

Pitiful, lonely, watching the black,
needing, wanting that Xanax maybe a lot.
Tired, angry blisters on my feet,

Sweating from the scorching heat.
Cold and lonely walking in the rain,
My heart filled with so much pain.
Trying to escape reality,
I lost all respect, even my dignity.

Sometimes I didn't have a dime,
So, I stole and now I'm doing time.
In jail, locked away,
Full of regret to this very day.
It was like drowning in a septic tank
Always running back and forth to the bank.
My life became so full of shame,
The sad part is I was to blame.

Those Xanax gave me a bad reputation,
I lied and cheated without hesitation.
Trying to be cool, living in the fast lane,
Dear God, I've caused so much pain.
Robbing Peter to pay Paul, Lord so much stealing,
I stayed in trouble with some kind of dirty dealing.
Some things I did scared me to death,
Lots of time it was so hard to get my breath.

My mother, Dear God, how sad when I last saw her face,
I've been such a sad disgrace.
My husband, I thought I needed so very bad,
Dear God our relationship was sad.
My children, my sisters, I've hurt deep inside,
But I couldn't face the truth no matter how hard I tried.
My family and few friends couldn't get to me,
I was so lost, I could not see.

So many times I prayed to die,
How it hurt to see my loved ones cry.
I lost my soul, caused my destruction,
Please, look what happens from a life of corruption.
I really let others get to me, I lost my brain,
Xanax helped with the pain.

I've lost the man I married,
I've lost the children I carried.
I tried so hard to hide,
I carried so much pain inside.
To anger and revenge, I was a slave,
It all bought me to my grave.
It made me want to hurt, to steal,
Sometimes I could of even killed.

Mixed emotions were growing stronger,
I didn't want to live any longer.
I really thought I'd gone crazy,
Always tired and lazy.
Sometimes I'd sleep for days,
When I woke I was in a maze.
I violated my whole creation,
Living only in degradation.

For years I buried a lie,
Seeking to cover my silent cry.
It's a miracle I'm alive today,
I'm so thankful someone really prayed.
I ran from God for so long,
I honestly thought I was so strong.
I thought I could run and hide,
But Jesus' blood finally came inside.

He said I'll take your burden and give you my yoke,
I can put you back together even though you're broke.
Delight in me, I'll give your heart's desire,
And all your needs will transpire.
Nothing can separate my love,
No more fear from below or above.
One day I wept and cried,
I asked Jesus to come inside.

I have found the taste of His wonderful love,
To soar high as a precious dove.
God said, "Jane, stop living a lie,
confess your sins, or you'll surely die."
I confessed and found such beautiful freedom,
and one day I'll inherit His kingdom.
I thought I could never face tomorrow,
Until Jesus came, He took my sorrow.

He cleaned me up, He turned my life around,
Now my feet are on solid ground.
He took all stains of iniquity,
Today I have peace and tranquility.
All I did was allowed God to come in,
And He took away my sin.
I know in my heart I am truly blessed,
My past is in the sea of forgetfulness.

I have eternal life,
No more heartache, no more strife.
Jesus controls my life today,
Without Him there's no other way.
His wonderful Spirit lives inside,
Forever in Him I will abide.

The witchcraft spirit had me bound,
But Praise God, He turned me around.

Satan comes and tries to steal,
But he has no authority against God's will.
I get my needs from the Holy Ghost,
In my Lord, I proudly boast.
I'm covered by His blood, in a new direction,
With Jesus I have full protection.
My Lord has set me free,
I've found God's Victory.

He rescued me from the pit of hell,
In His grace I'll forever dwell.
He transformed and renewed my mind.
He has power over all mankind.
Today I give Him all praise,
Forever Holy Hands, I raise.
The heartache and suffering from my past,
There's no comparison to God's glory that will last.

By His stripes I'm truly healed,
On my head I carry God's seal.
Lord I know I should of been dead,
But your Son died for me instead.
He gave His life on the rugged cross,
So that I would not be lost.
Thank you Lord for healing my soul,
For saving my life and making me whole.
Thank you Lord from up above,
Thank you Lord for your precious Love!

****

TESTIMONY OF EDITH SUTTON

I was born on November 16th, 1927. Both of my parents were Christians. We went to Broad Street Methodist Church in Richmond, Virginia. I grew up there. When I was old enough, I sang in the choir. We went there until I was seventeen. My Father died in June of 1994. I had just started working at the Federal Reserve Bank of Richmond.

I got married in 1948. My husband was not a Christian. We had our ups and downs. In 1950 my daughter, Margaret, was born. In 1952 my son, Harry, was born. We were having problems. I left when my son was 9 months old. I couldn't take it any longer. I went to my mother's and went back to work at the bank. I was so blessed to have her. I started taking the children to Tabernacle Baptist Church. I sang in the choir and was baptized in 1957.

In 1965, my Mother remarried and moved to South Carolina. She married a Christian man she had known all her life. In 1968 she was killed in a car wreck. I felt that I had lost the only person that had ever loved me. I know that the Lord was with me, and that she was in heaven.

I remarried after being single for sixteen years. A girl at work introduced us and we hit it off right away. My husband and I went to Fairmount Christian Church and I rededicated my life to the Lord.

My husband died in 1984 with cancer. God helped me through. I had always kept my faith and trust in the Lord. My son lived with me and we helped one another.

In 1996, I had quadruple by-pass surgery and got along fine. They were testing me for a liver transplant when they found my blockage. By the grace of God and my church, family, and friends praying for me, I came through fine. My children didn't want me to be by myself, so my daughter, Margaret, and her husband, Woodrow, came to Nelson County and found a house large enough for us. I told them that we needed to find a church and when we rode by Ridgecrest Baptist, we decided to go there. We felt such warmth and welcome that we started there regularly. *Psalm 73:26 My flesh and my heart faileth: but God is the strength of my heart, and my portion for ever.*

****

TESTIMONY OF ANNA OGDEN HARRIS

I, the daughter of Clifford & Nolie Ogden, was born and raised in Nelson County. I have four sisters and one brother. We were brought up in a Christian home. (Mama told us we could do and say anything we saw or heard her say or do). I never heard a curse word in all my growing up years.

I started my Christian life in a Methodist Church. Miss Ruth Cox was my Sunday School teacher. (She is still living.) I remember learning the books of the Bible and a song, "Pharaoh's Army Got Drowned in the Sea, O Mary, Don't You Weep, Don't You Moan." Later we went to Oak Hill Baptist. (My daddy played Santa Claus there). I graduated and went to Washington, D.C. to work for three years. I joined Metropolitan Baptist Church. Here is where I found out what being a Christian is all about. I left Washington D. C. in 1949, came home and married James Edward Harris. We have four lovely children. (I am proud of all four.) I went back to Oak Hill and this time I joined. I stayed there until Oak Hill and Walnut Grove merged and formed a new church. (All of Oak Hill did not leave.) The new church is Ridgecrest Baptist Church. (My husband donated the grading of the lot to the church.)

I have been active in church most of my life, taught Sunday School and Girls' In Action, and was director of Vacation Bible School for about fifteen years. I used my husband's pick-up truck and put a camper top on it, to bring children to Vacation Bible School from all areas of Nelson County. I was also active in W. M. U.

I love my Lord and Savior Jesus Christ and am still active in church.

****

TESTIMONY OF IRIS ANNE HOLMES

I was raised in a Christian home with Mama and Daddy and three brothers. Every Sunday, Mama took us to Sunday School and worship at Ridgecrest Baptist Church in Lovingston, Virginia. I still attend there today. At the age of twelve, I accepted Jesus as my Savior during a revival service at our church.

About a year later, I lost my father to cancer. He was only fifty years old, and I was only fourteen. This was very hard on us emotionally. But my wonderful Christian mother held us together and always provided for us so that we never felt deprived of anything.

The next year, at the age of fifteen, I met the young man who is now my husband. We married at eighteen, and he is a true blessing in my life. The Lord blessed us with our first son the following year. Two and a half years after that, we had our second son. We planned on having more children, but during the next several years I suffered four miscarriages. I was confused as to why God let this happen. I became angry and my spirit was weak. I thought God had turned His back on me.

On September 12, 1994, God gave me a wake-up call. I was rushed to the hospital in severe pain, and learned that I had a tubal pregnancy that was rupturing, and I was bleeding internally. I was rushed into surgery, and I remember thinking as they wheeled me down the hall that I might never wake up. I knew my heart wasn't right with the Lord. I began to pray and continued to pray until the anesthesia put me to sleep. The Lord did bring me through that day. He saved my life, but most importantly, He saved my soul.

Ever since that day, I have felt a hunger and a thirst for the Word of God that I never had before. I lost interest in reading secular books, and now read inspirational books. I have learned so much since that day in 1994. I have been compelled to attend Bible studies at church, and the Word of God has been opened to me as never before. I feel the presence of the Father with me as never before. I talk to Him now as not only my Savior, but as my friend. I have conversations with Him while driving in the car, while doing chores around the house, just any time at all. And although I don't understand why I had to go through those rough times, He has replaced my anger and despair with hope and faith and the light of His presence. I have a wonderful husband, and our two sons, now ages seventeen and fourteen, are a real blessing in our lives. Our oldest is a gifted songwriter, and hopes to use his contemporary Christian songs in a ministry of some sort. Our youngest is a wonderful singer and a fine young man. I can see God's hand in their lives every day, and that is truly a gift.

Trust in Jesus and let His will be done in your life. Time is short. Give your life to Him. He will bless you and give you peace. May God bless you on your journey.

****

TESTIMONY OF CATHY LAING

First, I would like to thank my Savior and Lord for releasing me from the power of sin and translating me into His glorious Kingdom of light. I'm thankful that He will never give up on us even when others do and that He has given me this opportunity to let people know that He is a healer of broken hearts.

My testimony is one of healing, not physical but emotional. Scars so deep that only the Holy God who created me could see. For we have a compassionate High Priest who is moved with compassion by our infirmities. (Matt. 9:36)

I grew up in a single parent home, thankful that my daddy made provision for me and my two sisters to be in church. It was in my early teenage years that the Holy Spirit began to tug on my heart. He showed me that I was a sinner, lost and without hope, apart from Jesus and His monumental sacrifice on the cross. I responded by walking down the aisle and asking Jesus to save me, then later was baptized.

Circumstances changed in my life, and sadly, church was not a part of it. Unfortunately, many years would go by as I went through life still doing things my own way. Even though I know now that the Lord had His hand on me all those years, (Matt.18:12) it wasn't until 1984 that the Lord allowed me to come face-to-face with the reality of near death. I remember begging Him not to let me die. I developed a severe infection after my daughter was born, which put me in the hospital with two surgeries. As I lay in bed Easter morning still too weak to go anywhere, I remember so vividly the sermon I hears. It was all about the Christian life with no visible fruit. The pastor used these words, "If you think you are saved and your life shows no sign of fruit, you may be fooling yourself." Friend, I know God in His love and mercy had that message just for me! I can't tell how fast I got down on my knees, pouring my heart out to the Lord! I only know my life has never been the same since that day in 1984! Only God knew my heart back when I was a teenager, and there was no obvious remorse for the sin in my life. Was I born again in 1973? Only God knows. What I do know is that He never stopped searching for me, and that is so evident to me to this day! I'm thankful God uses every experience that comes into our lives to teach and to mold us into the image of our precious Savior. I can truly relate to *Hebrews 5:8. Though he were a Son, yet learned he obedience by the things which he suffered;*

As I have walked with the Lord, He has shown me that there is a vast difference in knowing Him as my Savior and having Him as my Lord. When the time was right, (God is never early or late-He is always on time) my Lord led my family to a wonderful church. The ladies in the church were doing a Bible study course by Beth Moore called, "Breaking Free", making liberty in Christ a reality in life. One dear, sweet lady invited me to be a part of this Bible study, knowing I was new to the church. Tears filled my eyes as I think of how the Lord used this Bible study to heal my heart and set me free! For the first time, I could see just how special I was. I didn't have to try so hard to win people's approval or to make people like me. When I think of all the tears I have shed in my life and the experiences I have lived, it is a tremendous comfort to know my Jesus was crying right along with me.

After this Bible study I asked the Lord why He had not healed me sooner. His response to me was so soft and sweet. "My child, you wouldn't let Me." So often we hold onto worries and burdens that weigh us down. Burdens that keep us from being all that we can be in the Lord. He is Worthy. Remember, the scars in His hands prove that He understands. He longs for us to be free. Jesus said in *John 10:10, I have come that you my have life and that you may have it more abundantly.* All hail the precious Holy name of Jesus! Forever in His service.

****

TESTIMONY OF DIANA FORTUNE LANTZ

This is my testimony of how God has worked in my life. I was eight when I accepted Christ as my Savior. I remember it as if it were yesterday. We lived in Toano, Va. There was a revival at James River Baptist Church, and we all went. After the preacher had finished his sermon, he gave the invitation. I felt the need to go up and give my life to Christ. It felt as if someone was pushing me. I was so scared, but I made the move and went up. My three older brothers went up, too. A deacon of the church took me in a room and told me the plan of salvation. Later, all four of us were baptized. I remember that was a wonderful day for me, too. As I got older and started to date, I would remember that God was always watching me, and I never wanted to hurt my parents. I always wanted them to be proud of me. I know I have not always been or done what is right in my life, but I do know that without God I would never have made it.

When I had my two children, I prayed to God and thanked Him they were healthy. I told Him I knew He had only lent them to me and that I would try and bring them up to love and serve Him. Sometimes I think I failed God in my promise to Him. All I know is that I trust God to answer prayers and to keep His promise, to never leave us or forsake us. I will never stop praying for my family, that all of them will come to know the Lord. He has always been my help in time of trouble. One of my favorite verses is in Psalm 34:17 *The righteous cry out, and the Lord hears, and delivers them out of all their troubles.* I don't know how anyone could live without God. He is always there when you need Him. There are so many that say they are Christians and love the Lord, but never go to church or give Him any thing or any time. So many people have God in their head, but not in their heart. When you love the Lord you want to serve Him. They put their husband, wife, kids or other worldly things before Him, or they can't find a church that preaches what they want to hear. We need preachers that preach God's Word, not what we want to hear. Being a Christian is not an easy life, but is the best life.

I thank God for giving us to Mom and Dad. Most of all, I thank God for giving us Jesus. God bless all.

****

TESTIMONY OF LINDA DAVIS

I was raised in a Christian home. I was taught Bible stories as a child and went to church, Sunday School, sang in the choir, prayed, read the Bible and read devotionals. I believed in God and Jesus Christ all of my years growing up - in my *head*.

Even though things seemed to be going okay, there was something inside me that knew all was not *really* okay. I really wanted to be married no matter what. I had become engaged to a man that I knew, deep down, was not "the one". There were several "signs" that I just ignored. Then, one day, I broke off the engagement. I finally realized that things were not right and he was not the answer. I got on my knees and prayed to God and asked Him to take over my life - that I could not make it on my own. (I realized years later that God had saved me from a mess. Even though I was not walking with Him before that prayer, He was watching out for me. It takes years sometimes to see how God works, but it is always for our good.)

Next, I found a church where I could grow. I learned what it meant to have a personal relationship with Jesus Christ and accepted Him not only as my Savior, but also my Lord. I now knew Jesus in my *heart*. Making Jesus Christ Lord of our lives is not easy. We, as humans, especially me, like to be in control of everything! But, we need to yield to the Lord and let Him handle our situations. Also, it is easier to hear God's voice when we are *quiet* and *listening* and *waiting* on Him! The Lord is faithful through all the good times and hard times; when we do not listen and when we do listen.

A few years ago, I felt God calling me to a music ministry as a Christian soloist. I left full time work to pursue this. Since that time, there have been many times of doubt, struggling, and many questions. I have had several opportunities to sing, however, my schedule is not full. The opportunities are sporadic. But, even though I don't understand, I know a God who does understand and knows what He is doing. I have learned that nothing on this earth is about us, it is about Him and His glory.

As Christians, we will not be exempt from pain and hurt and sorrow. We do have the hope and knowledge that He is with us through it and working it out for our good, His perfect will, and His glory. Then, we know that we will have joy in the end!

****

TESTIMONY OF DOROTHY M. FORTUNE

I, Dorothy M. Fortune, wife of Dabney Haywood Fortune, was saved the third week of August, 1967, on a Wednesday night at Oak Hill Baptist Church, Lovingston, Virginia. Jerry Falwell of Lynchburg, Va. was preaching a revival meeting there.

I didn't have much of a background of going to church at all. I had attended a little here and there. I was going to Rockfish Valley Baptist when I met Haywood and his family.

My mother-in-law, Odie Fortune, wrote me a letter after I married her oldest son, in 1964. She told me she loved me and was praying for me to get saved. At first I was angry at her. I tore the letter up, but I couldn't throw it away. I know she had a great deal to do with my getting saved - her prayers.

How I thank God for giving His son to die for a wretch like me, and saving my soul. He died for everyone; if only they would accept Him as the atonement for their sins.

Haywood got saved a few days after I did. The devil placed this in his mind, if he went forward, what would people think? You see, his mom thought he was a Christian. I knew better. Though I wasn't a Christian, I had some idea of what they were suppose to be like and Haywood did not fit that description. He was a very jealous person and we often fought and quarreled over it.

We lived in a house but it wasn't a home. Just a little while after we were saved, we were at a meeting in the old dorm building in Lovingston, where the social services are now located. Again, Jerry Falwell was preaching a revival. That night we went forward as a family and asked God to help us have the right kind of home for our child. We had one child, Darlene. That was the beginning of a home, not just a house where three people lived. God has blessed us beyond our expectation. We'll praise Him as long as we live. There is no life on earth like the Christian life. Plus, we have hope in the hereafter.

****

TESTIMONY OF A MUSLIM WHO ACCEPTS JESUS

My life began in the land of Egypt, where most of the people serve the religion of Islam. A minority are in the ancient Coptic church and a very few are Roman Catholics.

Evangelical Christians are the smallest group.

I was born in a well-to-do family of well-educated Muslims. They wanted me to have a good education so they put me in an English school run by nuns. They warned me not to associate with any Christians.

However, I found good qualities in my Coptic friends that attracted me to them. One day they invited me to go to a church with them. When I entered the church, I sensed the presence of Jesus and felt He was saying, "Come to me, my child," but I responded no further at that time.

I had everything in life: money, power and position in society, but nothing satisfied me. Greediness, anger and emptiness were always there.

I thought perhaps that in marriage I would find satisfaction and fulfillment, so I got married to a Muslim man. But he was very abusive, and eventually left me. Our one-year old son remained with me.

After so many years of struggles, hardship and trying to find true peace, one day I was walking down the street almost crying. I didn't know what to do or where to go. Then I saw a man whom I thought was a Coptic priest on the other side of the walkway, and felt an urge to talk with him. In Egypt, it is very dangerous for a Muslim girl to speak to a Coptic priest, especially in the street, but I didn't care. I crossed the road and started to talk to Him. He answered all the questions that I wanted to ask him and gave an appointment to meet him at the Coptic church three days later. I was inspired and uplifted during those three days.

When I went to the church, I found another priest who was greeting his congregation after the service. I asked him about the other priest that I had met on the street, but he said there was no such priest associated with that church. I was greatly disappointed and started to cry. The priest introduced me to the other two priests serving in that church. None of them was the priest that I had met on the street. I kept crying so the priest took me to his office to comfort me. He asked me to repeat over and over again the same story, of how I had met the unknown priest on the street.

Finally the priest told me, "Daughter, I don't know this priest. All I know is he must be an angel from the Lord who came to you and wants to use you. It's your choice to believe or not."

Six months later my mother discovered that I had gone to this Coptic church and she was very upset with me. When the priest learned of my mother's anger, he would not allow me to come back to the church again. He knew that my father had power to shut down his church.

A year later, a musician friend of mine invited me to join singing Christmas songs at her (Baptist) church. From the first moment I put my feet in this church and saw the Word of God on the screen, heard the gospel music, and saw the congregation happily singing, praising and worshipping the Lord, I felt dirty and sinful.

I dropped down on my knees, weeping and crying. No one in the congregation knew anything about me, but they all gathered around me, hugged me, and prayed for me. From this moment on I realized what was missing all my life. It was LOVE, THE LOVE AND FORGIVENESS OF Jesus my Saviour that fulfilled the emptiness in my life.

I was hungry and thirsty to know everything about my new love, whom I called "MY JESUS". After a while, my family noticed the change in my life. And as I became so quiet and soft spoken, they thought I might have become a drug addict. They hired two people to follow me everywhere, and also recorded my phone calls. That was how they discovered my Christian activities.

They locked me in my room, and persecuted me for six weeks. But my Jesus never left me. I was always sensing His presence, and this verse was always with me, *But whoever denies Me before men, him I will also deny before My Father who is in heaven.* They beat me with no mercy, called me all kinds of nasty names, spat on me, took away everything I owned but my soul, and stopped serving me food. As they were getting ready to kill me, this verse came to me, *Behold, I send you out as sheep in the midst of wolves. Therefore be wise as serpents and harmless as doves.*

Miraculously, I got out of my prison. When I showed them anger, became violent and used a loud voice again (my old nature), I started to gain their trust back. Bit by bit they allowed me to get out of the room (prison), and eventually out of the house and into the street again.

The first thing I did was to get hold of the pastor of the Baptist church, who advised me to get out of the country immediately.

God opened a great door for me to come to the USA. I learned that my former Muslim husband, who had abused me so badly and abandoned both me and my son for six years, was in the U. S. preparing to get married to another woman. I received a phone call from a friend of mine in America and my father was on the line. He heard the conversation and encouraged me to travel to the States to get revenge on my husband and put him in prison. My father thought I would be in the U.S. only one month and then come back to Egypt.

That was the way I came to the USA. After a lot of hardships, moving from state to state and hiding from the Muslims, miraculously I ended up at the mission. They embraced me and my son, and gave us shelter, food and clothing. Eventually they gave me a job, and sent my son to a Christian school.

In God's time I was baptized at a Baptist church, and there also I met a godly, handsome man who was to make all my dreams come true. After one year we were married, and he has been a wonderful father to my son and an awesome husband to me. God has been so good to us as a family. He blessed us abundantly and together we are expecting the fruit of our Christian love.

About my family in Egypt, I had to cut all communication with them. They are still looking for me to get me back to Islamic religion.

Now I have a new name. God gave me that name after I was born again and became one of His children.

As you read my testimony, please pray for me, as I serve "my Jesus" among my own Arabic-speaking people.

****

TESTIMONY OF PATRICK ORR

I was experiencing my second divorce in less than ten years. My wife and I had just failed in a trial period of only five days around the Easter holiday of trying again to make our marriage work. I saw the failure as totally my fault because I had started dating a customer from the grocery store in which I worked at the time and believed I was too much in love with this new person to go back and really make it work with my wife. My wife lived with her mother while I made up my mind and finally issued an ultimatum to me; either come back now and give it a chance, or forget it. I was torn between duty as a husband and my love for the other woman. Even as I told my wife goodbye and walked out the door and down the sidewalk in tears, I knew I was making the wrong decision to follow my heart. You see, I had been attending church with my wife before all this happened, and we had been through this with another couple who had become our friends. Yet, I had become a hypocrite in urging him to stay in his marriage when I wished to do the same thing he had done.

As I left my wife and walked out of her life, my first thought was to get consolation from my girlfriend. I had drove in tears to her house, but when I got there, she had no time for me. She had a P.T.A. meeting to go to with her family. She left me drowning in my tears on her porch as she flitted away to her P.T.A. meeting, leaving me wondering even more about how wrong my emotions and thinking were at that time.

As I drove out of her driveway behind them, my only thought was to get comfort for my aching heart. My wife, in our last meeting, had read excerpts to me from a book by a Christian psychologist, who had actually gone through a divorce and then remarried her ex-husband. Some of the things she had read made sense because they were Bible-based, even though God seemed far away from me. I remembered what the preacher had said about God's Word being truth. I felt that if I could only get to church on that Monday night after Easter and pray to God to relieve my heartache, somehow that would soothe my guilt and hurt. But of all nights to be closed, the church I had been attending was locked up tight as a drum.

My panic then made me think about the book my wife had read me excerpts from by the lady psychologist that very night. If I could only get a copy of that book, I thought, maybe reading that book would give me relief. After searching the two bookstores at the mall, I gave up. In despair, I sucked up my tears long enough to buy a fast-food dinner to take home, but the drive home to my apartment was a blank. All I could think about was how miserable I was and useless to everyone, how my life was making everyone else's life miserable.

As I sat down to eat my cold burger and fries, I began heaving with grief from within. I asked myself, "What use is my life, to me, to anyone?" Just then a thought came to me, which I had never entertained seriously before. I could take my own life and in one action set myself free from my grief and from the pain I was causing others. I was ready to do it. I had the necessary tools in my apartment. But just as I got up off the floor where I realized I had sunk in my grief, and determined to carry out my self-proclaimed sentence, something miraculous happened. I heard a voice speaking to me somewhere inside. It was a voice I recognized right away. Jesus called my by my name. He said, "Pat, I know the pain you're going through, but if you'll just give your life over to Me and trust Me with it, I'll show you what I can do with it, things you've never dreamed of before." Right away my tears of sorrow and grief turned to tears of joy. Somehow ,I knew He knew me better than I knew my own self. Right there by myself on my living room floor, I turned my heart over to Jesus, and I've never been sorry since. I've been through two divorces, job layoffs and many other heartaches, but the One who knows me best, my Lord and Savior, Jesus Christ, has always been there with me to comfort and guide me through it.

Chapter Nine

ANOTHER WONDERFUL ANSWER TO PRAYER

Jeremiah 33:3 Call unto me, and I will answer thee, and shew thee great and mighty things, which thou knowest not.

    David, our pastor, used to always say people are not grateful for the rain. Whenever it started to rain, he would go on the porch, or stand in the rain and praise the Lord.
    We had been having a time without rain and our grass was dying. As we came from church, after prayer meeting, I said to Byrd, we should have prayed for rain, and she agreed. I never thought of it again, until last night. Then I prayed for the Lord to please send us some rain. I woke up and as I looked out I saw that it had been raining all night, and it was a gentle rain. Praise the Lord, the rain continued all that day.
    Dr. Henry just called, and the conversation confirmed what the Lord had shown me. My neighbor wanted to buy our place. I am still praying. As I have always said, when we want His will, He will not let us make a mistake. They have agreed that Eric and I could stay in the house as long as we lived. That would give me extra money for the publishing of the books. My dream is that each of my books would be printed in all different languages, and go all over the world. We will see if it is our Lord's desire, if so there will be no stopping it.
    This is the second time the Lord has stopped me from selling the house. He has shown me clearly that I am not to sell. He wants me to trust Him and Him alone, concerning the books. I am not to do it my way but His. That is what caused Cain so much trouble. He wanted to worship God his way instead of the way the Lord had told him. Our Lord so clearly showed Adam and Eve the way when He killed a lamb and

covered their nakedness with the skin, showing them that
...without the shedding of blood there is no remission. Heb. 9:22

Our pastor and his family are on vacation this week. To them the time will pass too quickly, but to us it will seem a long time. We miss them when they are gone. When I went to teach my class, I only had one person, Dickie. We had a grand time. The lesson was on Noah's Ark. I asked him to draw a picture of the ark as he saw it, which he did. I said, now read the scripture and see what the Lord said. Of course there was no similarity at all. We let motion pictures color our minds instead of going to the Word of God and getting the true picture.

Large classes are nice, but in smaller ones you can somehow get across better, as all enter into the discussion.

While I shared testimonies of Wanda Hasty and her son, Gary, in my last book, I must share this with you. Gary always picks me up at night to carry me to church. This story is about his little granddaughter, Victoria. They call her Tory, and she is about three years old. One day Gary and Wanda had picked me some vegetables out of their garden. Tory asked what was he going to do with those vegetables. He said, "I am going to take them to Miss Josephine." She said, "Is she going to eat them?" He said, "Yes". She said, "Well, let me bless them for her." And she bowed her head and said, "Lord, bless this food for Josephine, Amen."

When Tory's mother was a little girl, her father, Gary, was living a very wicked life, but since he became a Christian, his life has changed completely. He is such a kind, gentle man. Now, he can't praise the Lord enough.

Chapter Ten

GOOD NEWS ABOUT PAT MENDOZA

Romans 8:28 And we know that all things work together for good to them that love God, to them who are the called according to his purpose.

    In most of my books I have been following Pat Mendoza. When I first met her she was the Activity Director at Lovingston, Va. She left there to serve in Lynchburg Health Care Center. At this time she felt led to join the Rivermont Presbyterian Church. Her daughter was married there. As she was free now she felt that the Lord had something He wanted her to do. So on Christmas day, she went to this lonely beach with her Bible to seek God's will for her life. A large dog appeared and followed her everywhere she went, only to disappear when she got up to leave. She firmly believes that the Lord sent the dog to protect her.
    The Lord revealed to her that He wanted her to be a missionary. She was sure He wanted her to go to Mexico as her former husband was from there and she knew some Spanish. She told one of the ladies at the church her experience and the lady immediately told her she would give toward her support. Others joined in and the people at the church backed her. The Lord led her to Sports Outreach, a group who go over to Uganda. She went with them for two months and while there the Lord called her to be a full time missionary. Before I left to go away for the winter, Pat was home on furlough. She was discouraged and her health was bad. At first she didn't think she would go back. Then the Lord began speaking to her, so she was going back for one month to finish the first orphanage she had started to build for twenty-five orphans.

When I got back from Florida, she had already left. The following newsletter tells of some of the work. Self draws back from the hardships but her love for the Lord keeps her going.

UGANDAN NEWS

Children's Outreach Ministry Enterprise

Bombs, Hunger, War... Is there any GOOD NEWS??

Almost Finished!
Good news! It's almost finished...Boy aren't you glad our Lord didn't say that on the cross? What's almost finished? The orphanage for Pastor Isaac's "children" is almost finished. The pit latrine and cement floors are all that's left of construction; then, with the purchase of triple bunks beds and mattresses it will be ready for the first little occupants. Some of these children have never slept in a bed, let alone sheets and blankets of their own. Thanks to you people of Rivermont Presbyterian in Lynchburg, Virginia, for donating many of these items. If the money continues to come in for the orphanage, we plan to add more rooms for the ever-increasing number of orphans. Already several orphans from the war area, Gulu, will be coming to live in this new home. With the leftover bricks and money we will add one room next month for these children. The children are grateful and refer to you as their "Mums and Papas of America". Thank you all.

Good News! Three Teens saved!
Our very first camp retreat for the teens and three were saved! Yes, in the bush of Uganda fifty teens camped in leaky tents for three days. We all had a great time. Because the tents were in a circle, we decided to have twelve tribes of Israel as

teams and teach and preach about the Tabernacle and God's desire for us to be pure as He is pure. We had "manna" on the ground one morning (popcorn) and even had a "scape goat". At the campfires the teens tasted marshmallow for the first time. I never dreamed teens could be so fun! And it's a mystery to me why the youth love camping when their whole life is a perpetual camping experience!

Jennifer Starts School!
More good news! Jennifer is taking sewing lessons. Everyday Jennifer and baby ride a bodaboda, or bicycle taxi, to Main Street and sit at a sewing machine with Elizabeth, her teacher. I'm so proud of her! She is learning to create patterns using old newspaper and has just finished a dress for Baby Patricia (crooked seams and all). Baby Patricia is doing so well. Jennifer is a good mother. Thank you so much for your prayers for this little family. Jennifer and baby will move to the orphanage after her sewing lessons and sew for the children there.

Good News... "For Rent"
"For Rent....Includes pit latrine and electricity...only $90/month." So we answered the ad...It was a definite fixer upper. The last paint job was in 1952, when it was built! But it is perfect for our office. We have had two teacher training classes held there already and we have made it "children friendly" with many books and crayons and toys; thanks to my supporters who have generously donated these things. The children feel right at home in my office and it's a great way to get to know them personally.

There is so much, much more Good News I would love to share in detail; such as our C.O.M.E. ministry "missionaries" who are traveling to remote areas with the Gospel every week and even to some public schools. (Boy, we need these missionaries in the U.S. public schools, don't we?). And there is also the good news of my speedy recovery from infection following a wild cat bite (no, not a lion!). I owe my thanks to Bonnie Sue and Krista for their fast action.

There's even more but I'll save it for the next time. With all the bad news we hear daily, my prayer is you'll remember all God's Good News to His children. I have heard it said there are over 3000 promises in the Bible for those that love Him. Let's dig for that Good News! Here's one to start with:

1 Peter 2:9 But ye are a chosen generation, a royal priesthood, an holy nation, a peculiar people; that ye should shew forth the praises of him who hath called you out of darkness into his marvellous light:

>For His Children in Uganda,
>Pat Mendoza

Chapter Eleven

TIME FLIES

Psalm 46:10a Be still, and know that I am God:

One of the hardest things to do is to sit still and let God speak to us. As we sit there and try to be quiet, all kinds of thoughts dart through our minds. Satan will do anything to try to disturb us when we try to pray. It is said somewhere that Satan trembles when the weakest Christian is upon his knees. Oh, how much I long to know how to really pray. And yet, in spite of my weakness, the Lord still works for me and supplies all my needs. Philippians 4:19 tells us He will.

I had an experience this past Wednesday. We had a bad storm and lighting struck my air-conditioner. I had disconnected all my kitchen appliances but had forgotten the air-conditioner. (We are in a middle of a heat-wave 90-104 degrees.) I just committed it to the Lord and turned on my fan. When Ray came to pick me up for church, I told him what happened, and thought no more about it. I did mention fans and said I could use them. That night was W. M. U. and Brotherhood meetings. As I started to leave the church the men told me they would be over the next morning and put in a new air-conditioner for me. It is so good to have a good church family. Early that morning Oscar and Mark came over to take the old one out. David went to town and bought me a new one and by that night I had a brand new air-conditioner in my window. Only the Lord could do that. While He spoke to them, they had to listen and be willing to obey Him.

Of late I have been reading the books about The Little House on the Prairie. They tell about the things the early settlers were faced with as they went west. Are we strong enough to face things like that? I know I couldn't unless I leaned totally on the Lord.

    I remember the first time I cleaned fish, I had always said that was one thing I could never do. One day someone gave me some fish; we hardly had anything to eat. I cleaned those fish and was glad to have them. We never know what we would do until we are faced with it. One thing is sure, we can do all things through Christ who strengthens us. Philippians 4:13

BECAUSE

Because I have received kindness,
I have been spurred on to be kind.
Because I have caught the smile on another's lips,
I have found myself smiling.
Because I have known the joy of receiving,
I rejoice in giving.
Because I have felt pain,
I know what pity is.
Because I have seen Christ suffer,
I have had the courage to go on.

Mary Gemma Brunke

Chapter Twelve

OUR LORD FEEDS HIS OWN

John 6:48 I am that bread of life.

As I was fixing breakfast this morning, making toast, I noticed the price of a loaf of bread was a dollar and nineteen cents. That was the cheapest I could get. My mind went back to a day when someone told me we would live to see bread a dollar a loaf. I thought, how stupid can you get, that will never happen. Bread was selling for around ten or fifteen cents a loaf at the time.

I guess I live a secluded life. I have no TV and seldom turn on the radio. So until I was in Florida and listened to some preachers on TV, I never had heard of Y2K. Now I have ordered books and am reading up on it. However, before this book is published we will have passed that date. I don't know if there is anything to it, but to be on the safe side, I will prepare for it. I'm not worried because the Lord always takes care of His own. If anything does happen, what a wonderful opportunity to minister to those who are without Christ and have not prepared.

I don't think it can be much longer before we can expect our Lord to come in the air for his own. That is the one thing I am living for. Just think, each time we lead someone to the Lord, that soul may be the one to complete our Lord's Bride and we will be caught up to be with the Lord in the twinkling of an eye. Just think, no more sorrow, no more pain and no more tears. No matter what we have to go through here, it will be worth it all.

One of the things I stand in awe of our Lord is when I think of that meeting between THE FATHER, THE SON, AND THE HOLY SPIRIT. To think, before the foundation of the earth they chose me; might I say they chose everyone because He says whosoever will may come. If we don't know our Lord, He is not to blame. He will not force us to come to Him. The Holy Spirit is busy holding up Jesus to us. Jesus says in John 12:32 *And I, if I be lifted up from the earth, will draw all men unto me.*

If you have never come to Jesus, why not do it now? Tell Him that you are sorry for your sins and will He please come into your heart? You can do it right where you are. Our Lord is not willing that any perish but that all come unto Him. (2 Peter 3:9)

Praise the Lord, my neighbor, Jeff, asked me if he could cut some of my trees. He would give me one half of what he made from the sale of them. I told him to go ahead. I may not get enough to pay for the last books I had printed, but it will help some. I am still looking to the Lord for $1,500 that is due. The Lord has said in Romans 13:8 *Owe no man any thing, but to love one another: for he that loveth another hath fulfilled the law.* Had I not stuck with that, I would have been deeply in debt and would not have been able to pull myself out. It's always best to follow the Lord.

Well, Jeff just brought me the check. My half was $2222.20. Praise the Lord, I had $600 left for my needs. *Now unto him that is able to do exceeding abundantly above all that we ask or think,... Ephesians 3:20*

Chapter Thirteen

CHANGES ALL AROUND

Revelation 21:5 And he that sat upon the throne said, Behold, I make all things new. And he said unto me, Write: for these words are true and faithful.

    Talk about changes! Everything will be going along smoothly, and all of a sudden there will be a change. As I said before, Eric, my grandson, has moved in with me. He was concerned about me living alone. I knew that sooner or later he would need me. I told you he has prostrate cancer and has been given about six months to live. At the present he seems to be in remission and is working, which puts a little regularity in my life. When he comes home from work, after dinner we relax and play several games of Skip-Bo before going to bed. Bringing all his things created quite a problem as my house was already furnished. However, we are trying to sort through his things and mine, keeping the best and saving the rest for a yard sale this summer.
    It has been a hard winter and there has been quite a lot of snow and ice. I have missed quite a bit of church. The cold gets to me and I find myself holding my jaws and having to put a nitroglycerin tablets under my tongue to relieve the pain.
    One Saturday between snows, Eric took me to the Beauty Shop to get a permanent. It really lifted my spirits as my hair looked awful. Having all that time, I should have finished my book, but kept putting off writing.
    Eric's work faded out so he had to go back to Washington, D.C. to work. We worked out a plan. He was to stay in Washington until he made enough money to get caught up with his bills. I was to take a plane and fly down to

Florida and he would drive down later and work there. So I flew in, and lived with my son, Tommy.

Tommy had gotten Eric a job working with his former boss. Eric was to be on the road, going from job to job checking on the superintendents. Some week-ends he could come to where I was and sometimes he would have to stay on the road. Tommy was is working in Orlando, and would probably be there through April. He did not know where he would be sent from there.

To get back to my story, Eric took me to Washington, and I stayed two nights with my son, Mark. Then Eric took me to the airport to fly down here. Nicole met the plane and took me to Tommy's home. She takes me to so many places, between her jobs.

I must tell you about my trip on the plane. There were two stewardesses and one steward. All were very good. I have flown many airlines but this was the best ever. One of the stewardess seemed to take a special liking to me. I had to have a wheelchair to get on the airplane. She took me to seat number eight. It was supposed to be a section for three people but she gave me the entire section. She went and got me two blankets to keep me warm. It was twenty-four degrees when I left Washington. They soon served a continental breakfast; not long after that, they brought us a snack. I then asked the stewardess if she could help me to the restroom. She helped me up and took me to the first class section and then as I came out she resettled me in 1st class and brought all my things to me. They had a wheel chair waiting for me when Nicole met me in the airport. They took me to her car in the chair. I left Washington at 8 A.M. and arrived in Ft. Lauderdale at 10:30 A.M. It makes trips so much more simple when you go by air.

Chapter Fourteen

THE UNEXPECTED BIRTHDAY PARTY

2 Corinthians 9:7 Every man according as he purposeth in his heart, so let him give; not grudgingly, or of necessity: for God loveth a cheerful giver.

    The day started like any other day. Angie was going to school and she took me to the library so I could check out some books. As she was going on an interview, she had dressed up. When she came after me, she said, "Nannie, we are going to a birthday party." When I asked her who it was for, she said, "Her name is Irene. She is always helping nurses when they do not have the money to pay for their books."

    As we went across the street, I saw a large catering truck outside. We were ushered to a large room and the fellows from the catering truck brought in all the food. They served food from one end and the other end was for drinks and fruit. There were around forty people there.

    Irene was a lovely person with a great sense of humor. I felt I had known her all my life. She was so much like my people. She looked much younger than she was. This was her ninety first birthday. She is the same age as me!

    Irene was a wonderful help to those nursing students. Often the Lord sends help in unexpected ways as the following story tells.

SUBJECT: IS YOUR HUT BURNING?

    The only survivor of a shipwreck was washed up on a small, uninhabited island. He prayed feverishly for God to rescue him. Everyday he scanned the horizon for help, but none seemed forthcoming. Exhausted, he eventually managed to build a little hut out of driftwood to protect him from the elements, and to store his few possessions.

But one day, after scavenging for food, he arrived home to find his little hut in flames, the smoke rolling up to the sky. The worst had happened; everything was lost. He was stunned with grief and anger. "God, how could you do this to me?" he cried. Early the next day, however, he was awakened by the sound of a ship that was approaching the island. It had come to rescue him. "How did you know I was here?" asked the weary man of his rescuers. "We saw your smoke signal," they replied.

It is easy to get discouraged when things are going bad. But we shouldn't lose heart, because God is at work in our lives, even in the midst of pain and suffering. Remember the next time your little hut is burning to the ground----it just may be a smoke signal that summons the grace of God.

Chapter Fifteen

ALL CREATURES GREAT AND SMALL

Genesis 1:24-25 And God said, Let the earth bring forth the living creature after his kind, cattle, and creeping thing, and beast of the earth after his kind: and it was so. 25 And God made the beast of the earth after his kind, and cattle after their kind, and every thing that creepeth upon the earth after his kind: and God saw that it was good.

    Molly and Samantha are very special. One day Nicole and Tommy were at the market and there were three little puppies for sale. Nicole picked one out and they paid twenty-five dollars for her. They took her home and named her Molly. Now she stays with Angie. When I came down here last year she was a little puppy, but this year she has grown so much. She is a beautiful dog. Angie evens brushes her teeth! Did you know they have special toothpaste for dogs? Molly's is beef-flavored. Wouldn't it be wonderful if we could get toothpaste that made us think we were eating a steak? We wouldn't have any trouble getting the children to brush then. Angie and Joe take Molly to the beach fairly often; she is treated like a child. She is black and white, her hair is curly and her legs and part of her body have spots like a Dalmatian.

    While Molly can only get out when they take her places, as they live in town, Samantha has a large place to run. Jeff and Kathy found Samantha at a dumpster; just a little thing starved for food. They brought her home and she soon filled out. My place is in the mountains, and she has twenty acres to run on. Kathy lets me keep Samantha when I am home and she cares for her while I am gone. Sam, our nickname for her, is tan and now has quite a bit of gray, since she is 9 years old. She is still frisky. When she wants to get in the house she can jump as high as the doorknob. She chases her tail so we will give her attention. Eric enjoys Sam. He will ask her to talk to him and Sam really tries. When Eric lights a cigarette, Sam will go to him and make hissing sounds like she is disgusted with him.

David, my pastor, loves all kinds of animals. I always tell him that he comes to see Sam and not me. He has a darling dog, also. One day David was going to school, on a real cold morning. He saw this little deer in the middle of the road. She was laying there and couldn't get up. He stopped his car and stood there and talked to the deer for quite a while. He patted her on the head. Then he went around to her back still talking to the deer; he finally picked her up and laid her on the side of the bank. On the way home, he planned to get the little deer and take it with him, but the deer was gone.

I have a friend named Ridgley who owns a farm. She has lots of goats, some sheep, a donkey and chickens. It is really a treat to be there when it is feeding time. She beats on a metal drum and the animals come from everywhere. She milks the goats, makes butter, and sells the eggs that her chickens lay. She is a multi-talented woman. When the sheep are sheared, she takes the wool and puts it on the spinning wheel and spins it. Then she knits sweaters, shawls, mittens and caps. One day she went to the fair with one of her milk goats. She would milk her, with a Bible on a table, and would tell the people that just as she had to milk that goat, they needed to get in the Bible, as it is the milk of the WORD. (1 Peter 2:1) She does it more because she loves animals than for anything she gets out of it. She is financially able to take it easy. But there is no joy in just laying back and taking it easy.

Chapter Sixteen

ANGIE'S GRADUATION NURSING SCHOOL

Proverbs 16:3
Commit thy works unto the LORD, and thy thoughts shall be established.

Angie has gone to the airport to pick up my return ticket. While I love it here in Florida, I have a special love for my home in Virginia. One thing I know, I will not leave until her graduation. Wherever we went she took her book with her to study. She has worked in between times to make enough money to meet her needs. She is a precious one.

Joe, too, is in school, studying something in law enforcement. When he graduates, they plan on getting married. Both are to be commended. We went over to his parents' home for dinner Sunday evening and had a lovely time. Tommy had taken me to breakfast that morning. This coming Sunday is Easter and we are again going over for dinner.

Last Sunday, while we were sitting at the table, Angie asked me what it meant to be born again. Joe had just made the remark that he had gone to church, but it was the wrong one. He is of a different faith and, had gone the night before to Angie's church. Christopher, Joe's father, said, "There are no wrong churches." That is when Angie asked the question. It was so wonderful to be able to explain the simple plan of salvation to them all. While it is easy for us to ask the Lord to forgive us our sins and come into our hearts and save us (it has to be with all our hearts), it cost Jesus everything. First, He had to leave His wonderful home in heaven and live among men in this sin-laden earth, yet He never sinned. He knew when He was facing the cross, that He would die for our sins. Knowing that His Father would have to turn His back on Him, He called from the cross, "MY GOD, MY GOD, WHY HAVE YOU FORSAKEN ME?" Then He said, "IT IS FINISHED", and bowed His head and died. They took His body and put it in a tomb. BUT PRAISE THE LORD, THE GRAVE COULD NOT HOLD HIM. On the third day, He arose from the grave and revealed himself to his disciples. I believe Mary Magdalene was the first to see him.

    I have gotten a new skirt and sweater to wear for Easter Sunday. While most people had new clothes for Easter, I rarely did. I look back over my life and see where our Lord brought me from poverty to, you might say, wealth. While I have my Social Security check, it is amazing the things I get to do and the many gifts of expensive clothes that are given me. Imagine a poor person getting to fly to Florida for the winter. ONE THING IS SURE, YOU CAN'T OUT-GIVE GOD!!! HE GAVE HIS BEST FOR US!

    A missionary was down by the river bank when she saw a woman with two children walking toward the river. One child was lame and the other one was a perfect little girl. The missionary asked her where she was going, she answered her and said, "I am going to the river to give my daughter to my god." The missionary asked her if she was going to give the little crippled child. The woman said, "I would not give a crippled child to my god; only that which is perfect." Could we do less to our God? I was reading in Leviticus that we are not to offer anything that is blemished to the Lord.

Chapter Seventeen

SITTING UNDER THE WORD

Luke 24:45 Then opened he their understanding, that they might understand the scriptures,

      As I was sitting in my Sunday School class listening to the teacher and the comments of the people, how my heart ached when I listened to them. Several Sundays ago we were studying in Ezra, and they seemed outraged that Ezra had told the people to put away their strange wives and children and come back to God. Their sympathy seemed to be with the wives and children. On the surface Ezra seemed to be cruel. But when you get deeper in the lesson, you see that God saw that those wives and children were deep into idolatry and were drawing these men away from the true and living God to idols. Also, the class failed to see that when the Lord told Ezra to give that message to the people, he did much praying and weeping before the Lord. Ezra had a hard thing to tell the people.

      Today's lesson was on Nehemiah, when the Lord had to correct the wrongs the Jews had done of taking advantage of the poor Jews and profiting from it. What upset me so, the class didn't seem to sense at all, that the Lord wants us to come up a little higher. He longs so much to give us the abundant life. He has sent His Holy Spirit to indwell our bodies, "the temple of the Holy Spirit", to enable us to live that abundant life. That should be the normal Christian life and is available to all who want it. In Galatians 2:20, He tells us that if self is put on the cross, He will love through us. It is not I but Christ. As we study the word, we may see what the Lord is really telling us. Lord, help us look fully to you in all our lives.

Chapter Eighteen

STICK TO THE WORD OF GOD

1 Corinthians 14:40 Let all things be done decently and in order.

Many thoughts have been going through my mind this morning. It seems to be thoughts that have come into my mind from time to time, but now they seem to be intensive. I hardly seem to know how to put them into words. So many books coming out, warning Christians of what to be aware of. They are good Christian novels, to turn the Christian to good rather than bad reading. I have gone through two books and really enjoyed them. In doing this, I find that many times the reading of the Word of God somehow is not as vibrant as before. The reading of great men of God begins to be laid aside for the good but not the best. Dare we put our whole trust in the Lord or do we not? We read many books on how to be a better Christian when all the while the Lord has told us if we "will" to be better Christians, and yield our lives to Him, the Holy Spirit will bring about the changing of our lives. Sometimes we try too hard. We try to carry the burden rather than "let go and let God", which is really the only answer.

I am thinking of Amy Carmichal. The Lord used her to do a great work in India. She had a place named Dohnavur, where she rescued many boys and girls from the evil of the priests of the temples. They used them as prostitutes for their desires. She took in little ones that had terrible scars in their lives and brought them out through love, always holding them up to the highest. So many of them grew up to truly honored the Lord.

It was said, if you wanted to work with her, one of the

things she required was that you never read a novel. She held her workers to the highest, also. Dare to be a Daniel, dare to be an Amy Carmichal. Let go and let God. We must be willing to listen to the Holy Spirit who will do the work.

When we read so many things, our minds sometimes get confused and we don't know what to believe. We need to stick to *Philippians 4:8 Finally, brethren, whatsoever things are true, whatsoever things are honest, whatsoever things are just, whatsoever things are pure, whatsoever things are lovely, whatsoever things are of good report; if there be any virtue, and if there be any praise, think on these things.* So our minds will be stayed on Him. It is in the "will" that the battles are fought. Do we "will" to control our own lives or do we "will" to let Christ control our lives?

Chapter Nineteen

THE LORD HAS IMPLANTED THE HOLY SPIRIT IN EACH PERSON AS HE IS BORN AGAIN

John 14:17 Even the Spirit of truth; whom the world cannot receive, because it seeth him not, neither knoweth him: but ye know him; for he dwelleth with you, and shall be in you.

Jesus did not start His ministry until He received the power of the Holy Spirit, received in a bodily form of a dove. The same Holy Spirit took Him into the desert to be tempted. He was tempted on all points, yet He yielded to none, therefore, He can help us when we are tempted. Remember, He was man, also. He understands. *There hath no temptation taken you but such as is common to man: but God is faithful, who will not suffer you to be tempted above that ye are able; but will with the temptation also make a way to escape, that ye may be able to bear it. 1 Corinthians 10:13*

After the time of temptation was over, remember He never yielded. He had no sin, yet the temptation was as real to Him as any temptation is to us. Yet many times we fall, because we do not call on God to deliver us. Jesus quoted God's Word. Do we know enough of His Word to throw at the devil, or in our hearts do we want to yield? Satan makes it strong. Jesus did not ever try to heal anyone until He healed them in the power of the Holy Spirit. A believer is never passed by Satan, but Satan will try his best to influence them, to drift them into believing false doctrine. When Jesus heals we are made whole. Holding on to false doctrine or superstition will not make us spiritually whole. We cannot have the fulness of the Holy Spirit, as long as we hold back anything from yielding to the Lord.

When they saw what Jesus did, they even admitted He could be the son of David, but brushed it aside and claimed He healed by the power of Satan. How do you react when you have clothes hanging on the line and it breaks, and all falls to the ground? How do you react when you have been working on your car all day and nothing seems to help? When a real temptation floods your life, do you seek God to help you overcome, or do you dwell on it and entertain it in your minds? Does it bother you at all that your husband, wife or child, would go straight to hell, if something happened to them and they were not saved?

Do we have a hunger for the Word of God? Do we read it through the week or just on Sunday morning? When a little one is born, it automatically cries for food, if it is a healthy baby. When we have life in the Spirit we, too, want His word, and as we start with the milk of the Word, we soon want the meat of the Word. Was there ever a time in your life when something came up that you knew you couldn't handle, and you cried out to the Lord for help? ... *God is our refuge and strength, a very present help in trouble. Ps. 46:1   ... Whosoever shall call upon the name of the Lord shall be saved. Acts 2:21*

Chapter Twenty

DIARY OF THE WEEK OF VACATION BIBLE SCHOOL- 1985

July 10, 1985 Today I spent the morning getting my flannel graph together for Bible School. Jeff was taking his time doing a few things. I sure got upset with him, so I left at 2 p.m. to go to Amherst. Just as I was going out, I met Steve, my pastor at the time, coming up the road. He had some fliers for Vacation Bible School. I told him about Jeff. He always seemed to know what to say, as he remembers how he was at Jeff's age. He must have prayed for me, because all the way to Amherst and back, the Lord dealt with me about my attitude. I asked the Lord to forgive me and to help me to leave things in His hands. When I got back, Jeff had his work done.

Brenda came by, but didn't stay long, as she felt bad and wanted to go to bed. I managed to spend sixty dollars on groceries, gas, gifts, and crafts for Little Church. I picked up some pizza for supper. Ashley is with us this week. While I was gone, he and Jeff washed the dogs and after supper we went to prayer meeting. Ashley came to Little Church with me. Jeff and Kathy went to prayer meeting.

I'm rather tired now so will sign off. Oh, yes, I got a swing for the children. Wonder of wonders, working with children again and loving every minute of it.

July 11, 1985 I got up at 6:30, read my Bible and prayed until 8:30 a.m., then decided to clean the house. It sure needed it, especially my bedroom. Brenda traded me a single bedspread for a double one. My bed looks so good with a spread that fits. Jeff got up at 11:30 a.m. and Ashley at 12 noon.

This afternoon, I cut out around twenty little lambs for

the children for Bible School, then started looking through the National Geographics for a picture I could use in place of one I lost. After quite a while of that, Brenda came by and ate supper with us. Ashley fixed my sidewalk and Jeff cut the grass and went to career night at a reality company.

After Brenda left, I discovered I could use a picture from the first lesson to fit in. Ashley drew a couple of scenes for my lesson.

Steve called and wants me to come over at 8:30 in the morning and keep the children while he takes Teresa (his wife) to the doctor. As I have to be there anyway, to clean my rooms for VBS, it worked better for me to go then.

I am rather tired; have had company steady for almost 2 weeks - Scott - Donnie - Nancy - Tommy - Brad - Angie - Betty - Norbert - Ann Dwyer, a missionary, Eric, Ashley - April - Chris. Eric and April, his girlfriend, come tomorrow and will leave Sunday with Ashley. I don't expect any company next week. That will be good, as I will be teaching all next week.

I was in Atlanta for 10 days before with Angie, Nicole, Stephanie, and Tommy. Went out several times with Jimmy while I was there and once with Jeanette; she brought me a pair of glasses.

While I was there, I met a Muslim couple. The girl was so good to us. Also met a black girl. She took us to the zoo. After that the Muslim girl took the children and me to her apartment. The children got to swing, then she took us to dinner. Her husband worked with Tommy. Well, I am rather tired, so had better get to bed. Love you, Lord.   Sign off.
Mary J.

July 12, 1985   It stormed all night, lightning and thundering, pouring down rain. Just got up at 6:30 and had my quiet time. Looked at the clock. I was supposed to be at Steve's at 8:30 and it was 8:00 o'clock. Time just flies when I am with you, Lord. I dressed and left around 8:15. It was raining quite hard; you let it lighten for me, until I got there. The children were good and I got my S. S. lesson together, still have 5 lessons for Bible School to do. I got home around 5:30 p.m. I was so tired I fell across the bed and went to sleep. Brenda and Jeff came in and I never heard them, slept until 6:30. Then Myrtle came and rang the bell. She stayed until 9 p.m. I ate a tomato sandwich for supper and later another one. I must try to cut down , as I weigh 134 lbs. - most I have ever weighed. Lord, help me be so yielded to you that love will flow through me to others. Myrtle was lonesome and somehow I failed to fill that need. Please, Lord, remove the hard metallic tone from my voice when I talk to Jeff. I feel so selfish; you shower me with gifts. The car, Lord, 1984 Chevette, am I wrong for refusing to let Jeff drive it without me? I mean, am I being hard when I say, they cannot live here when they get married? And about money, Lord, you know I have more to spend than I ever did. When things break down, You always see I have enough to have them fixed. Then I seem so hard to Jeff. Lord, please take over and melt my heart with love for others. Firmness when it is needed, please, Lord, not hardness. Please go before and work things out with the little ones. I somehow feel that this is of you.

    Lord, thank you for the $300 Bobby gave me that was left over from the car. Help me to use it the way you would have it used. Lord, if I am to continue sending that money to Jimmy Swarggert the hungry children, help me hear from him by Tuesday. If it isn't to go there, then direct where it is to go. Oh, yes, thank you, Lord, for giving me that trip to Atlanta, especially stopping off in Charlotte, N. C. to see Glad. My what a testimony, when I asked her, how she would have me pray for her, she said, "Josephine, pray that I will always be obedient to my Lord. I have read my Bible through 76 times." Here that precious soul lying there, not able to move, feeling rather useless but always wanting to put her Lord first. Lord, I reminded her how she took me under her wing, always patient with me, always listening to all the burdens I poured out on her, only to get 5 minutes to read the Bible and have prayer with me. Little by little she made You very real in my life. And when she saw I was walking with you, she went on to others. I will always thank you, Lord, for sending her into my life. So many memories in these last 40 years. I will probably mention them from time to time, only, Lord, to give glory to You.

About 9 o'clock Jeff, Ashley and Kathy came in, we burned out the wax in their ears. How you do that is take a white cloth, tear a strip and wrap it around a pencil. Dip it in paraffin wax. Slide it off the pencil. Let it stay in the freezer until firm. Put one end into the ear and light the other end. As it burns, it pulls the wax out of your ears - weird, but it works.

When I came home, Jeff had the tractor, and was fixing the road. Doubt if I could have gotten back here, if he hadn't. He is a good boy. Guess I expect too much from him.

I will try and get up in plenty of time to carry Myrtle to the store, before Eric comes. I am signing off tonight. I love you, Lord, and may your Love be shed abroad in my life to reach others. Mary J.

July 12, 1985 Got up about 6:30. Had my quiet time and studied my Sunday School lesson. About 9:30 picked up Myrtle and we went to Amherst. Stopped by Coleen, got a hamburger, fries and a drink. I got home about 1:30 p.m. and put a roast in the oven, as we were expecting Eric and April. However, they didn't arrive until around 8 p.m. We all ate then. Roast, gravy, green beans, succotash and potatoes. After that we burned out Eric's ears. And talked awhile. Just as they were leaving to go to Brenda's house, Hazel Moon called. I am to pick her up next Sunday morning. It will be a 2 or 2 ½ hour drive each way and we have to be at church around 10 a.m. So I will have to leave early. I look forward to the missionaries coming, they are precious people. Monday we start VBS.

I pray You will keep Your hands on the little ones and give them receptive hearts. Please simplify the stories for the little ones. May they truly know more and more that you are alive, a living vital person in our lives, a real Friend. It is almost 12 p.m. so I had better sign off and get some sleep. Eric says he is going to cut down the dead tree in the morning. I hate for him to do it on Sunday. Lord, if you wouldn't have him do it before he leaves, change his mind. I will leave that with you Lord. Good night, M.J.

July 14, 1985 (He didn't cut the tree down.) I am extremely tired tonight, Lord. It was 12 p.m. before I got to bed, got up at 6:00 a.m. Had a couple of hours to have my quite time and go over my lesson. You were in my Sunday School class in a real way. Also, in Steve's message. Lord, both of us are worn out, but you have promised, that your strength is made perfect in weakness. You send the children of your choice, and please Lord, work out any discipline problems. May we have such perfect peace and love, that the children will feel it and react to it. You have promised to give me strength. And, Lord, I am looking to you for just that. Went back to church this afternoon and got the rooms ready for VBS then came home and studied for Little Church and it is time to go back. Please, Lord, let both Tricia and Becky learn something from the lesson and, dear Lord, give us wisdom in VBS. May each one of the teachers feel drawn to each other, and give us a real love for each other. Good night, Lord. I love you. Mary J.

July 15, 1985 Rough day yesterday, forgot to write in this book. 1st Day of Bible School. The children were precious, and, Lord, they really listened to the lesson. Lord, thank you for Joan, she really sees that things are running smooth, also takes on the mission story, plus hand crafts. Lord, help us to work together, that one doesn't have to carry the load. Lillian is precious. She helps us, Lord, to work out the singing step by step as we work out our schedule for the class. Be with each class, Lord; we ask not only for Bible School, but we long for spiritual results. Help us to present truth to the little ones. They are not too small to receive truth. That is when they need it. May real faith creep in their hearts.

May Joan come back to your house again. Give each teacher strength.

I picked corn, cucumbers and squash before going to Bible School today. Took Myrtle to Lovingston right after I got home. Laid down at 3:15 and slept until 4:15, then picked butterbeans. Storm came up. Jeff set the table for me and took care of several little things.

I canned 7 qts. of squash plus put down a 5 gallon bucket of pickles. Shelled butterbeans, got 1 pint for the freezer. Then I studied lesson, didn't get much out of it as I was to tired, so must close now and study some more. Please, Lord, may there be a rich fruitage for your glory. Mary J.

July 16, 1985 Almost didn't write tonight, just wanted to go to bed. Lord please show us the right way to teach those little ones. Put within us love, but also firmness that the children will listen to us. You arrange the schedule, Lord, the way you would have it. Give us spiritual results, Lord. Open the hearts of the children. Speak to Joan's heart to get back in church. Give all three of us a closeness that we will try and help each other. Lord, if there is another one you would have work with us send her, give me the right time for Henry to come in to play his guitar. My day seems to run pretty much the same. A little quieter today. Got up at 6 a.m. for my quiet time and study. Left for church at 8:15. The children were more restless today or felt like now they were used to us. They took more liberty, if only I had the wisdom to handle these situations. Several were really interested. Guess I want them all to listen and want the Lord. Tricia acted up outside today. Steve took her home, but she got back for the mission story. Keep your hand on her, Lord, and lead her in the things of the Lord. I got home around 12:30 p.m. After lunch and tending to my bills and check book, took a nap. Woke up around 3:30 p.m., studied until supper, then went out and pulled bean beatles for almost 3 hours. We can't spray as it is always raining. Did my dishes and took a bath, did some studying and now I am ready for Wed. End of day. Mary J.

Chapter Twenty-one

GOOD TO GET HOME

Mark 5:19 ...Go home to thy friends, and tell them how great things the Lord hath done for thee, and hath had compassion on thee.

I have jumped around so much, going from one to another of my children's homes. I am now at Bobby's in Richmond. I came to get some new dentures.

To get back to things, I came back to Virginia to my home on May 15th. My granddaughter, Robin came down to see me on the twenty-fifth of July and I went back with her. She carried me down to her lovely place over the Coan River, as the dentist doesn't work over the weekend.

It was such a refreshing time and all the grandchildren were there at their homes. David came down and stayed with Bob, so it was good to see him. He is Larry's boy.

I was at Bobby's three weeks before I came home. I am still having trouble with my dentures. I may have to go to a dentist here.

It is always so good to get home. I guess everyone feels the same. I feel the Lord has given me this home and I am to be a good steward of it for Him. I will never forget the day I was standing in the strawberry bed and my head was lifted up like a magnet and I told the Lord that all the land and the house was His, that is why I don't feel I have a right to sell it. My children think at ninety-one, I need to sell and move in with one of them, especially my daughter. I am not afraid to live alone.

Eric stays in Washington most of the time, but was here last weekend. Scott, my great-grandson, his wife Kim and

Courtney, my great, great- granddaughter, were also here.

Sunday was a lovely day. David Beverly took me to church. They were going somewhere afterwards so Carol took me with her. We all went to the Lovingston nursing home to see her aunt, Iva. Iva's sister came to church so she drove us to the nursing home. They were at lunch, so we slipped out and went to a restaurant to have our lunch. Frank, our choir director and his wife Edith, were there. So along with the lunch we had good fellowship. I had a hard time enjoying my meal as my new teeth are giving me so much trouble.

We went back to church. Leo came in a little later and told us that a drunken driver had been driving all over the cemetery and had done a lot of damage to it. He said that they drove over Sharon Morris's husband's grave. I am sure that Sharon was there today. I have not been able to get in touch with her.

I called about Byrd and they say she has been awake half the night and is still awake. You know the Lord may raise her up yet. She is a miracle woman. As she has been near death's door several times and she pulled through. She has nine children. I have asked them for testimonies, which I will include if they give me one. I spend a lot of time over there.

The Lord is so good to me. While I can straighten up things, my time for cleaning is over. Bertha Sites and her daughter came over and cleaned half of the house. They are coming over tomorrow to finish it. They will not take a cent. That is their love gift to me.

Chapter Twenty-two

THE MIRACLE LADY

2 Corinthians 5:8 We are confident, I say, and willing rather to be absent from the body, and to be present with the Lord.

It is now September 2000. My friend, Byrd, lived quite a few weeks longer than expected, before she died. I tried to be with her as much as I could and of course, there were some of her children with her all the time. Little Jimmy and his grandmother, Ruth, were there from Sunday night till Friday night. The children filled in each weekend.

Little Jimmy is Jimmy's oldest boy. He was born with some defects and is in a wheelchair. Chris is his second son. He has seven children in all. You could not ask for a prouder daddy. He has one grandchild. Jimmy sings with the Statler Brothers. Haywood is Byrd's oldest, child, then Wayne, followed by Maynard, Deanna, Brenda & Linda (twins) then Jimmy, Anna Marie, and Tony.

Byrd was such a loving, caring person. Her every thought was to do what she could do for others, even as she was dying, she still was thinking of others. One night she thought I was there. She kept telling me I must go get some sleep. So Linda made believe that she was me and that she was going to bed.

The day of her funeral, the church was packed, people standing in every available space; flowers everywhere. They had so many they carried all that they could down to the cemetery, had quite a few in the church and took so many to their home, and had the whole place covered with flowers. I have never seen so many flowers at anyone's funeral, even though my son had so many when he died of a heart attack, however they could never come up to Byrd's. They had asked that instead of flowers, donations be sent to the rescue squad or the hospice. I am sure many sent to them.

The day after the funeral, I got sick and by the weekend, I was put in the hospital and was there until the following Thursday. I am now feeling much better. The nurse is going to release me next week. The doctor put in for them as I live alone. It is raining outside now. Louise is coming to take me to get my hair cut. After I came home, Stephanie came down to help make up my diet. Did I tell you she has a beautiful little baby girl, Jessica? It was a joy to hold my little great-granddaughter in my arms. I would sing, "Jesus Loves Me" and as I sang and rocked her a little smile would spread over her face. I am sure she will be a blessing.

Virginia Breadlove brought Betty Robertson and Evelyn Strickland and Edna to visit me the other day. We had such sweet fellowship together. I love company! They took me out to lunch. The Lord is good to me. I have so many good friends. It is wonderful also how He supplies my needs. Many times the money comes before I am actually aware of the need.

At Thanksgiving, I am planning on going back with my daughter, Betty and granddaughter, Elaine, and will stay until January 12th, (2001) then I'll fly to my son Jimmy's home in Florida. I will be ninety-two on January 13th. I'll stay until around the first of May.

My, I have a wonderful Lord. I am especially thankful that He has given me a sound mind. ...*God has not given us the spirit of fear, but of power, and of love, and of a sound mind.* 2 *Tim. 1:7*

PART II

MY TESTIMONY OF JESUS CHRIST
by Mrs. Heang Oak Horm

Background: I was born in Battenburg, Cambodia to wonderful righteous parents.

The true story of my life is how the Lord Jesus Christ changed my heart completely. Many years ago, I suffered during the communist invasion in Cambodia, during those hard times I received many miracles that the Lord revealed in my life - that He is the only true and faithful God. I have memories of it all; even today I remember all the miracles, which the Lord had planned. Everything that He did amazed me in so many ways. I had never encountered anything quite like that in my life. The Lord put a burden in my heart to share my personal story with everyone He led to me, who have yet to receive the Lord Jesus Christ as their personal Savior.

I hope that by reading my testimony, it will touch someone's life that they may come to know the Savior like I know Him, personally, spiritually, and intimately. The power and the glory of the Lord, is the God full of mercy, knowing that it's not us who searched for Him, but it is He who has chosen us to be His children. It is the most amazing grace. I can't contain it or even compare it with anything else in this world. I am most thankful to the Lord for giving me this great opportunity to share my story of how the Lord became the Lord of my life.

I thank Mrs. Betty Dunnevant for helping me to share this story with you and I hope that you will be blessed by reading it. Before I begin with my story, I would like to start by letting you know about my family background.

I was a daughter of a fine carpenter; the most noble and popular carpenter in town. There were five children in all.

My parents loved all of us so much. They weren't rich, but they were kind and generous to us and to their neighbors and friends. They were well known in town as the righteous people. They had the heart to love the people all around. Friends and neighbors were always around the house. They all knew them by heart. Both of my parents worshiped Buddha because of my ancestors and my culture and tradition. For many generations they had always believed Buddha, even until my generation. I worshiped Buddha, also. We were living in the darkest time of our lives. We never imagined what was the right way, so we just followed the faith of our ancestors.

In 1967, I was about seventeen years old. I got married to a young man who was ten years older than I was. He captivated my father's heart. He was a very young, handsome professor, who was kind toward my whole family; he obeyed my parents as if they were his own. In 1968 we had a son, Tann Veja Horm.

At that time the country started to have a little fighting on the outside of the country in the rural area. The Communist had their armed forces to start a war. A year later, I was pregnant with another child. Then, my husband volunteered to be in the armed forces for the country's protection. The whole country had closed down the schools when my husband joined. He was sent to Vietnam for training. I was about seven months pregnant.

My daughter, Sourneat (Sor-ne-ed), was born when my husband returned from Vietnam. After that, my husband was transferred to different areas to serve the country. I stayed with both of my children and with my parents as normal. Between 1970-1974 the fighting continued, one after another; my children were both little and my husband was always away from home. We were only together every once in a while, because of the armed forces he served.

Later on he became very ill, and in 1974 he asked to

resign from the armed forces. So, he came and was with us at home. We all took care of my husband until he got better. He tried to open a class in the area, once in a while, to teach students at home, making some money.

In 1975, the communist group, the Khmer Rouge, fought in every area of Cambodia. They invaded the whole country, took over the cities, and forced all the residents to leave their homes. They were to go out and start a new community in the rural areas. They were to start cultivating the soil to grow the rice as the main crop and start cleaning the woods to get the place ready for farming. We all went without anything that we owned. We just had a little bit of food with us. Our homes and belongings were taken over by the Khmer Rouge. They allowed us to stay out in the rural areas. They created a new group and community there for us. They separated us from my parents to a new town. My husband, my children and I were sent to stay in the new town, outside of the city. We were afraid of the new area because we heard rumors that the Khmer Rouge searched to kill anyone who was in the profession of teaching, armed forces, doctors, lawyers, etc. Anybody who was educated in any way, they were to eliminate, even the movie stars. I was worried and scared while I was doing my duties. Nights and days my husband and I were worried and scared of dying, especially my husband. We hardly slept at all. Every morning we were to line up so they could count us for roll calling for their records. My duties took place at a different area from my husband. They set up a cafeteria to serve meals to all the laborers. We owned no pots and pans, plates or spoons. We only possessed our strength and energy for work. After our work was done we were lined up to get our meals every day. My husband was so frightened and he had no hope to survive because of his position as a professor and his rank in the armed forces. He was the leader of the armed forces and that made him a true traitor. He didn't trust the authorities; he fled from there alone. I was scared and frightened. I didn't know what to think. I couldn't go with him when he begged me to because my daughter, Sourneat, was very ill. I thought we had no chance to escape. If I go with him we all might die because of the children, but if he went alone at least my children might have a chance to survive.

The head section leader of our group went to meet with the authorities of the communist concerning my husband's escape. I didn't know whether he was alive or dead. The authority requested my kids and me to meet with them. They called me "a traitor's wife". The leader of my section and the town leader (the people who ruled over us) had a meeting in this case. They said if we take them to the authority we know for sure that they will kill them all. The section leader refused to take us to the authority man. My older brother, Ouch Bouy, who was the second child, stayed in my section, too. He was tormented knowing that they were going to kill me for my husband's crime. He cried days and nights over my life. He cried like one would for a dead person, "My sister, this time you will not be alive. They're not going to let you live! Oh! My dear sister! You are going to be killed! Who's going to save you? Oh! My sister. Because her husband ran away, he had done wrong and now she's going to be in his place of trial." He kept on crying like that.

The section leader and the head of the town had him calm down. He said, "That's all right, I'm going to try to rescue you and persuade the authority leader. Maybe they will listen to my pleading." I was so numb at that time, I was frozen, I didn't know whether my husband was dead or alive. I kept thinking about him so I wasn't concerned for my own life. My section leader went and pleaded for my life. He had made an oath that if my children and I disappeared from that village they were going to kill him instead. So, he put his life on the line for my kids and me. I was relieved and didn't worry a bit about dying, because the section leader had saved us. He was so wonderful to us; we never knew each other before. (But I greatly thank the Lord for making his heart tender for us. Only He alone can change a man's heart.) He took care of me as well. He provided my children and me with food to eat every day. Things with farming that I didn't know how to do, he did most of them for me. He treated me as if I was his sister, his own flesh and blood. His wife was the same way, too. They both were so wonderful to me. He brought us some fish to eat. He always kept his eyes closer to us because he was afraid that my husband was still alive and would come back for us and he would end up dead. He really did trust me. He said, "If you tried to escape from me, I will surely die before my family!" He said, "I don't know why I trust you so much to risk my life for you!" Then I said to him, "Don't be discouraged, you risked your life for me, I will risk my life back for you, too. You saved our lives; I will not let you die because of me. And to leave your wife and children, too." I lived very close to him; he always kept his eyes on me. We stayed in a little shed next to his home.

The Lord gave me wisdom to be brave. Then the head of men in the town lost his wife. She had died. He had great feelings toward me. He called the elders in town to come to propose to me in marriage. I said, "Sir, I can't accept a new husband, my children are still too young and very small. I want to wait until they grow a little bit." He couldn't settle for that so he went to the authority leader. That was the man that convicted me earlier. That man requested the authority for me to see him, (I wanted to give thanks to the Lord once again, I didn't know Him then, but I had so much wisdom from the Lord." As I was working, the section leader came up to me, "You must get married with the authority man. You must come with me right now!" I replied to him, "Please sir, do not make me go, here I have written him a letter, just deliver it for me and if he refuses to agree with me in the letter, then you can think it over again." The section leader then took my letter to the authority man. In that letter I wrote:

Dear Mr. Authority, Sir, you have done so much for me in the past that I could not thank you enough. You have saved my life when I was supposed to be dead, but you rescued me. I look up to you as if you are my father. You have given me a new life. I felt like I have just been born all over again because of you. My life had just begun. Why did you want to love me, if you had already gave me a new life? I trusted you as if you were my father, who gave me life. I didn't just love you as a brother or a husband, but I lifted you up as a father, one who gave me life. How could you let me love you in such a way? If I had already respected you in such a way in my life."

Those words had touched his heart. It made him take pity on me so deep. Then he said, "That's alright, I will wait for another opportunity." He took all of his words back and his demands. He went and told the head authority or his leader about that. His leader said, "Yea, tell me whatever you want, I will demand that this woman take or accept you." (That was what the Lord had done in my life when I didn't know Him yet, but He recognized and knew my broken heart, my deep sorrow for my husband. That was the burden and I had put all of my love in my children.) I went back to work as usual.

A few months later, they sent my children and me to a new place; it was a village. That was the place for the rest of all the widows from different areas around the country. The communist leaders put us all in one place together. My children and me were staying at that place, and they allowed my children to be with me. At that place I was troubled but I thanked the Lord that I had my children with me. I went to work in the morning and in the evening I spent time with them. We were together every night. That took the worries away from thinking about my husband. The other widows had lost their husbands through death, also.

A couple months later they took three families including me, and sent us to a far away town near the mountain. The place was called, "Town 64". It was far away from home, near the mountain called "Mountain Tap-Day". When my parents heard that, they knew that it wasn't good. They wondered why they only chose us three families out of all those people. They forced us into the military truck with guns behind our backs. They pushed me into the truck. Then they put me in one very quiet place, like nobody was there. There weren't any signs of farmers or anything. We were supposed to start a new life at that place. They built many small cottages in those woods. They put me along with another lady who had smaller children; her name was Souy. I usually called her "Sister Souy" because she was older than me. The two of our families shared that one small cottage there in the woods. She had four children. The two older sons were far away from her. She had the two smaller ones with her. I had my two children, my son, Tann Veja, seven, and my daughter, Souneat, who was only five.

Souy and I knew each other from the other camp. That place was very quiet when we got there, and it seemed as if people were there at one time before they all vanished (died), then only empty camps in the woods. They started a new cafeteria with many other widows that I have never met before. They were brought there from many states. The appointed one lady to be the head of that cottage, to rule over the entire widows. They had the top leader who rules over all, which were the communist head leaders, the Khmer Rouge. They ruled over that one lady. Anything going on in that cottage place, she would report to the top leader of the Khmer Rouge. At that time I became really homesick. I missed my hometown and my parents. I went to work just like everybody else everyday.

One day they took both my children away from me and sent them to different places. They used to sleep on each of my sides at night, one on the left and one on the right of me. I lost my mind. Even if I had to work day and night, my children were with me and that would make me very happy to have that communion with my children. I would be so glad to go to work everyday and every night. But at that time I was so exhausted; I was drained out. I felt depressed; I was going insane. I started to hate myself, not care about anything about myself and I didn't think about anything at all. I felt unbalanced. But I still went to work as I normally did everyday. My son, Tann Veja was very far away in distance. Souneat was a little closer to me. She could walk to me, but she was so little. At nighttime she snuck out of her camp and came to sleep with me. Each day when I lined up for my meal, I hid a small portion of my rice in my handkerchief for her each night. I knew that when she ran to me, she snuck out while they were serving their meals. So, she skipped each meal to be with me. They had a small cafeteria for the little children, separate from the adults. While they served the meal, the leaders of the children weren't paying any attention to them because it was their break time, too. My daughter hid in the empty well until it got dark, then she came to me. I was troubled in my heart very deeply. No food to eat, only one small portion of rice that I hid for my daughter which was my share.

The discipline: One day I told my roommate, Souy, "If my daughter keeps on running to me like that, one day she will surely die. This little bit of food will not be enough for her everyday." Then I started to hit her and told her, "Don't come here any more! I do not want you to run to me like this. You should stay where you are and eat enough food that they served and sleep and go to work. If you still do this I will not love you anymore." I hit her and she replied to me, "Mother, I am not hungry; I just want to be with you, to sleep close to you. Just to sleep close to you is enough for me. And I will go to work; please, mother, stop hitting me." That night she stayed with me until the next morning, she went to work just like everyday. She still ran to me every night nonstop. The other children had nobody to bath them. All the children went to work and went straight to bed. When my daughter came to me, I bathed her and I held her in my arms every night.

One day they ordered me to a new location far away. I was worried, knowing that my daughter would definitely come to see me. The road that she came was along the high hills. The rivers were on each side of the hills. They were for the good use of the rice field, to make the rice grow better. Those two rivers were filled with deep water and the high hills were for the people to walk on. My daughter went along that road every night to come to see me. That frightened me greatly. I was supposed to work in the filed at that new location far away. I told Souy who went with me, "Sister Souy, if my daughter comes to look for me and I'm not there, she will keep on going. And if she keeps on going, she will drown in some river for sure." Souy thought that I was losing my mind. I knew that she thought I was insane. She kept trying to cheer me up by saying, "Heang, everybody else is in the same situation as we are. Why aren't they thinking like you? Why aren't they thinking this way? What makes you worry so much? You surely will go crazy if you keep on worrying this way! If she can't find you at the cottage one of these days, she will go back to her place."

It was because of love that we were thinking the same thought; I knew that this is the amazing testimony of the Lord up until now. I knew everything now; before I was wondering and questioning things. I was questioning my life, when I didn't know what was going to happen to me. I thought that my daughter would find me. My daughter will find me that night. I hid my food away for her. Every night, that was my hope that my daughter will come to me. One day while it was raining really hard, she was on my mind so much that I wanted it to be a reality. I wanted her to come to me that day. I kept on looking out of my tent telling Souy that my daughter will come to me; she shook her head.

Sourneat's story of that same day. "I got to my mother's cottage. I found no one there. It was really quiet, not like every other day. When I hoped I would see her, she was there for me, but on that day it was different. As I looked around the cottage, it was empty. I saw her "sarong" (skirt) hung up on the window. I grabbed that sarong and I cried out loud in despair, "No! Mom. Why are you gone? Where is my mother? Mother, where are you? Where have they taken her? Please, mother, come back..." I cried until a lady who lived nearby heard my cry and came to me. She came over and tried to calm me down. She told me where my mother went. I lost my mind. I went back to my old place. The other children looked at me weird. The lady there took me by the arms. She tied me up to the tree and put red ants all over my body. She let me sit out in the hot sun for hours. Later on I saw my brother. He told me where my mother was. It seemed as if I was dreaming the way things went. I ran away looking for my mother. In my heart I was determined to find her until death. I had to find her. She was my life. There was a big rain storm. The lightning was hitting very hard and very loud. The thunder was very loud, too. As I was walking all by myself in the middle of the field on a big hill...."

Back to my mother's story. I hid my food for my daughter just like I always had. It was raining very hard and it was very dark. I kept looking outside in the rain. Every time the lightning went out I could see outside better and when the lightning stopped, it was dark again. We stayed in the barn, me and Souy and the other families. There weren't any walls at that barn, just a roof over us. We could see far off. It was out in the open. The rain started falling very hard. That barn held about five to fifteen families. We all slept inside our mosquito net. I whispered to Souy, "Sister Souy! My daughter will try to find me." She said, "Heang, please don't be crazy. You see how far we are? She cannot come this far! Please stop thinking about that." She kept trying to comfort me. She pitied me, she thought that I was losing my mind for sure. I was so sure that my daughter would come and find me. I didn't know what those feelings were, that I was so sure that my daughter would come. Then, I sat inside my mosquito net and I waited and kept on looking outside. I saw the lightning. I looked at the hill in the distance. The fields were filled with rice and water. When the lightning struck again I looked outside in the light, then, I saw a small skinny figure on that hill far away. It was moving to the direction of the wind, as it was blowing. The storm was shaking that figure back and forth. Then it got dark again. I went and told Souy, "There's my daughter!" I sat there and stared and stared and stared out there at that figure until my daughter came closer and closer to me.

   After she came off that hill, I went out in a hurry. I didn't know why my daughter found me. It was very dark that night. How can she know that I was in that barn? I kept wondering, questioning that. I wondered and wondered many things that went on in my life. Then I went out and embraced her in my arms. I brought her inside my mosquito net. I whispered to her so nobody could hear us. That was against the authority. I bathed her secretly in the little pond that had some water nearby. I wrapped her up in my little towel and brought her up into my mosquito net. I then gave her that small portion of my rice, which I had saved for her to eat.

   I was filled with joy at that very moment. I couldn't compare it with anything else. In the morning I took my daughter back to her place in the dark night. I then came back to my place with joy. Later on they moved us back to our cottage. One day my daughter came to see me and I told her, "My Daughter, you cannot survive just from eating one small portion of rice everyday. If you love me you will stay and eat with them. When there is time that you really miss me then you come to me. If you don't miss me that much just stay the night there." The place where she stayed was like a barn. They slept like animals, one over another. They all slept on the floor. They just went to bed without taking any bath. They were treated like animals, because the girls that watched them were young themselves. At night the leaders went to their bed and the children sleep on the wooden floor. They slept on each other like they were pieces of logs. They were squeezed onto each other. They pinched each other at night on the arms or the legs. The bigger one would hit or pinch the little one to make room for them.

    They suffered during bedtime and mealtime, especially the smaller children. So, during this time, not anything was normal. I often wondered about these things. Each night my heart cried out to my daughter. Since then she did what I said. Sometimes she came to see me and sometimes she didn't, she spent the night with them. There were times when her leader wasn't too strict; then she came to me. Other days when I waited for her and I didn't see her for a couple days. I got scared as I was working. I talked to Sister Souy, "My daughter hasn't been around, I wondered if maybe she has drowned?" Sister Souy said, "Heang, you should ask permission to go and see her, wherever the children work." So I went to where she worked. Then I saw her there.

    Later on she didn't come again, I went to see her, but she wasn't there. I asked her leader where she was. She said, "Your daughter went to the hospital, because she had been bleeding out of her belly." I got scared when I got back. I told Souy my daughter was sick. Since Souy was an older woman, she was able to share with me about my daughter's symptoms and what it meant. She knew more things than me. I said, "What if she's bleeding out of her belly now. They sent her to the hospital." She told me, "Heang, that hospital has no use for your daughter. I know there is no medicine or anything. She would just sleep there and they wouldn't provide her any food or medicine." Then after work I asked the leader if Souy and I could go and visit my daughter in the hospital. When we got there, I saw her in bed. Her belly was swollen very badly. It was red and it stuck out of her tummy. I was frightened and I asked Souy, "What should I do, Souy? What kind of medicine do I need for her?" The hospital provided only the rice powder. That rice shell they grinned and mixed with sugar, but not too sweet. That was their medicine. Then I gave up my hope on her. Souy said she could die from that, because she knew that kind of sickness was lack of honey and sugar. The bleeding and swelling would stop. She couldn't live without the sugar or honey. That tumor will not be healed. I had no hope and I asked Souy, "Souy, where can I find sugar? We live by the communist authority; we can't have anything. We could hardly taste any salt. The soup that they prepared for us was already cooked just enough for that meal. We lived like prisoners. I drained myself from worrying about my daughter.

I was scared and afraid of her dying. I slept in distress. No hope. I was a mother; even sugar, I couldn't afford to get for my daughter. I worked everyday. Something as little as sugar, I couldn't get for her to help her to live. I cried, I sobbed each night. I didn't know where to get help. No hope in anything. Because we lived in the prison, we couldn't go anywhere on our own. Then I could only cry; tears rained down my cheeks, they soaked my bed each night. I was broken-hearted from losing hope. That day I got home I cried myself to sleep, scared of losing my daughter. I saw her sick in bed and I knew what could cure her, I couldn't get for her.

The First Miracle One morning, they appointed me to go find some vine to tie the cows together for farming purposes. They appointed sister Souy and me to go together.

Every couple had a different kind of job. Some had to go fishing. Sister Souy had actually requested to go with me because she knew what kind of vine came from certain types of tree that was the best kind. They let her go with me, besides, she was the one that could climb trees. So, we went to search for the vine together. On that morning, I went to find that vine with Souy. I didn't really understand about the vine at all. I just went along with Souy; she knew more about the vine that they wanted us to find. I just did whatever she told me to. Every morning we went to the mountain and tried to find the vine. Later in the evening we went home. In the morning they gave each of us a piece of rice cake for that day of work along with some food. Everyday we did the same routine. Every morning at 4:00 a.m., they lit the lantern and looked at our faces as they checked our names on the list. Two people paired up as they got in line ready for work. But that one morning was a miracle that seemed peculiar to me. I still thought of my daughter laying there in the hospital bed waiting to die.

    We went out in the direction to "Mountain Tap-day" which was very far and a lonely place. There were many thickets nearby. There we should find the big strong vine. We walked toward the big road, which led us toward that mountain everyday. On that big road there were many people from different directions. They all merged from many small roads to that big road. Everyone had many different duties and with many expectations. They came from different towns. Many weren't under strict authority as we were, because they were real farmers. They didn't lack food as we did. They lived their normal life with plenty of food in many varieties. They were all together with their families. Husband and wife and children were together. One group was all just men. Some of them were beating on their cows to make them move faster on the road. As Souy and I were walking along with them, we blended in the crowd. That is when the amazing incident happened that I could never forget. I heard a lot of noises from the cows and the people along the road. I tried to get out of their way. Souy went ahead of me because of the crowd. I heard the cows, the buffaloes, and many voices of men that went along the way. The men said, "Hoy! Hoy!" as they were beating on the animals to make them move faster. Then suddenly, as I was walking and running at the same time just to keep up with everybody else, I heard a voice of a man calling behind me as I was moving out of the way. He called me loud enough in the crowd that I could hear him, "Lady! Young lady!" At that time I didn't know what made me answer to that strange voice. I shouldn't have answered him because in my group we didn't know any men at all, neither could any man visit us. But, I stopped and I yelled back, "Are you calling me?" That voice came behind me again. I couldn't see who he was because it was too crowded and it was still dark. Everyone put on "krama", a handkerchief we used to wrap around our head. We bumped into each other in all directions. I couldn't turn back. While I was walking I yelled back to him, "Are you calling me?" Then that voice answered me closer and closer, "Yes, I'm calling you lady!"

   As I was walking and I turned my back at the same time, he grabbed one of my hands and he handed me something in the package. It felt very warm as it touched my hand. Then as I tried to avoid the cows coming my way at the same time, I just lost the man without seeing his face. His voice sounded like an older man. I was frightened as I was walking, wondering what just happened. I called "Sister Souy!, Sister Souy!" As I got that stuff in my hand, I quickly turned around trying to look and see who he was. I couldn't find him anywhere. At the same time I was trying to avoid the animals and the people who were walking on that big road. I just knew for sure that it was a man. As I was calling on Souy, I was afraid that I might lose her. She waited for me up ahead and said, "Heang! Heang! I'm over here!" I started to explain to her, "Sister Souy! You wouldn't believe what just happened to me. Somebody just gave me something a few minutes ago. Did you hear him calling me?" She wasn't that far away from me, I would've expected her to hear him calling me, too. She said, "No, I didn't hear anyone calling you. All I heard was the men calling for the cows along the way." Then I told her, "Sister, someone gave me something; it's still very warm." I handed her the package. She started to feel it and see what it was, as we were walking together very quickly. It was still dark outside around five or six o'clock in the morning. We continued to walk very fast and we talked at the same time. We had to speed up so we could get to the mountain quickly by daylight. I told Souy, "Wait until it is daybreak, then we can open the package and see what's in it." As we were walking until the daylight came, we started to find a place to sit down. We opened the package very quickly and inside were still very hot marinated huge shrimps with honey. It was so delicious looking food just like from heaven. The shrimps were soaked with honey sauce. As I saw that, Souy was so surprised to see that and I was, too. Sister Souy said, "Oh, Heang, I can't believe this. Who gave you that? Maybe he got you mixed up with some other lady? Maybe he accidentally gave you that package and thought that you were someone else?" I felt so guilty after she had said that and I said to her, "Sister, I wondered that too! I wondered why did I say to him, "Are you calling me?" There were many women around me, too, but he seemed very sure of it and no one answered him, but me. I replied to him, "Are you calling me?" and he said, "Yes lady, I am calling you!" He seemed convinced that it was me and he handed to me the package without even looking at my face. I was walking very quickly in that crowd, and then I lost him." Sister Souy said, "I'm confused, why did that man give it to you and you didn't even see his face?" I did wondered that to myself, why was he so sure that it was me when he didn't really see who I was. That question stuck in my mind all those times. As she opened the package she said, "Oh, Heang, this is the food that you need for your daughter. This is the medicine needed to cure your daughter's belly. I don't understand why this man gave you this, the one thing that you really needed." I was so overjoyed I couldn't wait to bring it to Sourneat. "How did this man know what I needed? Sister Souy, I can't share with you any of it, because my daughter needs it." I told her. She said that we will take this to her this evening. She will recover from bleeding. She just needed sugar in her body.

    I was overjoyed; I couldn't wait for us to return home, and take it to my daughter at the hospital. As I got there my daughter received it with joy. It was just like it was food made from heaven for her. We both were filled with joy. We laughed and we were happy together. She ate the whole thing. I returned to my cottage and work, like any normal day. I kept wondering about myself that I was a Buddhist. I worshiped Buddha, and why didn't I pray to Buddha for help? There were many times that I suffered, but held it inside my heart. And my heart was overjoyed when I got home. I was hoping that eating that honey would heal my daughter.

    If she had that she would've been healed. She wasn't completely cured, but the swelling was better and the belly was still red. The doctor sent her back to work a few days later. She came to see me. Sometimes she couldn't come, sometimes she came like I had told her before. One day she told me, "Mother, mother!" She was crying while she talked. She was soaked with tears. She said, "I always eat rice by itself. A bowl of soup had to be shared with four other children. They were all bigger than I was. That would taste great with my rice, but I couldn't fight them. Sometimes the soup spilled because they were fighting over it. Nobody gets to eat it. So,

I only eat rice by itself, Mom. If I got a piece of salt to eat with rice that would be so nice. I just wondered how great that would be, to be able to taste something with rice, Mother?" At that moment tears were rolling down my cheeks from feeling my pain with my compassion toward her. She said, "Mom, how can I eat just rice by itself for the rest of my life?" I just told her, "It's going to be alright honey, in a little while we will find some salt. It's going to be alright." I told her that to stop her from crying. She returned to her orphanage place. A few days later I was scared, when they appointed us to go to work at the other place, further down. The top leaders commanded it, for all the women that had no children under five years old. Those women with their small children, they held their babies each night. They could take them to the childcare while they were at work. Souy had a baby boy, three years old.

The Second Miracle The women with no infants were considered as if we were single. They sent us to anywhere that they pleased. They treated us like we were in the military. So, they sent me to sign up for that field. I was to go with them. The leaders didn't even know where they're going to take me. They just told me to sign up for that. We were to go to another state. As I was already far away, I never saw my son's face. And now my daughter, too. Why should I live? The next day as they got us in line for that journey, I didn't go with them, I just stayed at home and cried.

They all prepared themselves for that journey. When they missed me, they came to get me, but I refused to go with them. I said, "Go ahead and kill me, I'm not going. If I go my daughter will be dead. So, I will not go!" They thought I was insane because I wasn't afraid of the "Anka" (the people in the authority of the Khmer Rouge, the communist gorilla).

They all went in the big army truck. Those were the women without small children. Then the leader of my group, he came to talk to me, "Oh! Heang, I cannot be responsible for your problem. You have refused to cooperate with the "Anka"; this will cause big trouble. This is not up to you, whether you want to cooperate or not. If you refuse to cooperate you will have to go to the "Anka" yourself. I cannot be responsible for you. I already reported to the top leader of this matter. They all wondered about you. I will not die for your sake. I cannot be responsible for you because you have betrayed the "Anka", you went against them. You didn't obey the law."

From that moment on I was broken, but I didn't worry about dying at all. I was just so broken for my daughter and my son. I thought to myself, if I went with them my daughter will definitely die. If I go with them my daughter's life is ending. I decided to go to the "Anka", the leader of the communist groups. They were the leaders of the widows. As I got there, they mocked me in all kinds of ways. The couple that I went to see was very young. The husband was known to be the most dangerous man who killed many Cambodian civilians. They just had a little child about a year and a half old. She just carried her in her arms. They lived in that big house with plenty of food. They had maids, and guards were always around them. They lacked for nothing. They made me sit and wait for them downstairs under that big house. As they came down to see me, they were laughing at me like I was insane, saying, "We heard that you don't want to live? Is that right? Those women who were signing up for that new journey who devoted their lives with the "Ana". But, you refused to cooperate with us instead. That made it easy for us, that you're saying you want to die!" His wife came down with the baby in her arms and sat there and listened.

All of their guards carried guns with them. They were protecting the leaders of the "Ana". All the leaders were staring at me. When the leader said that, I began to have great wisdom and I said, "Oh, my brother, I didn't refuse to cooperate with the "Ana", when I refused to go with the rest of the women;

it was because I have my daughter. I love my daughter very much. And I'm sure you understand because you have a baby, too. She is still a little child, she's only five years old. Every night she ran to me. In the morning she went back to work under her leader. She had never missed any of her workdays for the "Ana". No matter how many times she ran away to me, but she never missed a day of work. And she's only five years old. She is like an infant still, she still sleeps with me through the night. And if I went along with the other women to that new place my daughter will end up dead. I need to explain to you "Ana" very clearly of exactly what happened here. It's the truth." The leader's wife had compassion and pitied me when she heard about my little girl and she started to ask me questions, "How old is your daughter? I told her, "Five years old, sister". The "Ana" wife was younger than me, but I called her "sister" with respect because of her power over me. One of the guards recognized my daughter from what I just described in my story. He was the guard who watched every night on the road where my daughter ran away each night. He said, "Who is your child? Was it that little child that had a funny haircut? I couldn't tell whether it was a she or a he because of the hair cut." I answered him, "Yes, sir, that's my daughter with a funny hair cut! I just used my knife to chopped her hair down because she never bathes over where she is and she had so much lice on her head. I just cut her hair short so I could wash it better." And the guard said, "I have rescued that little girl from drowning almost every night. I saw her drowning in that river. I just picked her out of the water so many times." The guard said that in front of the leaders of the "Ana". The leader's wife heard that and she said, "My goodness, she is just a child!" That made her husband stop mocking me. His wife had deep feelings for my daughter. I began to plead to them, "Please, brothers, sister, if my daughter was big I wouldn't be here pleading to you or go against your will like this. I would be so happy to do anything you asked me to for the "Ana". I didn't think that she would run to me like this. And she wouldn't be thinking this way, if she were older, she would be happier to go to work. She wouldn't be thinking of me. And I wouldn't think of her so much either. We all would be working for the "Ana" with joy and wherever you send me I would not refuse to go."

I told them all that and they were filled with compassion. His wife pitied me and my daughter; she said, "She is still too small, she's too small. If you send her mother away she will die for sure." The guard witnessed her running to me each night. He saved her from drowning many times, he said, "If I hadn't been there and saw her she would probably drowned and be dead, that little girl." The leader was used to having the power to kill anybody he wanted to. He wouldn't tolerate anyone who went against the "Ana". Instead he let me go home and report to work as normal. But in my heart I was prepared to be killed. I thought to myself, they were supposed to kill me. I knew that I was supposed to die because I was wrong. Why then didn't they kill me, that was my second question. He said to me, "My sister, why don't you just return back to work as you normally do." So, I went back to my place, but I didn't believe that I could get out of that so easily. I knew I was going to die one of these days. I knew my punishment was death; no one was able to forgive me. That was supposed to be as an example for others. If they forgave me someone else would try to do the same. They had such great power, so much power that they would never forgive me. I just waited for my turn to die. If it isn't today it will be the next day.

Souy was crying over me with the deepest sympathy. She said, "You are most definitely going to die. Oh, sister Heang, you should never have refused to go. If you had gone with them you could have your life and you would be able to see your daughter's face. But since you have refused to do as they said, if they don't kill you today, one of these days they will kill you without you knowing it. Now, they're not going to kill you because they don't want to stir up trouble with the people in the city." I was so brokenhearted, so humbled. I have lost my hope in life. As I came from work I just sat still. When the nighttime came, I went to bed. I heard the wind blowing during the night. I still went to work daily but in my mind I lost hope in life, knowing that one of these days they would kill me, because I had betrayed the "Ana".

One night when my daughter came over, she slept with me as usual. I bathed her in the little pond nearby as usual. I wrapped her up in my little towel and I brought her into my bed. She whispered to me, "I'm so hungry, Mom. If I get some rice and salt, wouldn't that be so delicious? I never had any food to eat when I'm with the other children, they always gave us a little bowl of soup to share with the others. I could never fight for food. So, I just ate the rice by itself all the time. If I could just have a little piece of salt to go with the rice, wouldn't that be so wonderful, Mom? That would taste so great." I was deeply touched by what she said. If I were dying that would be all right with me. I would be so scared in losing my life as losing my daughter. My son was so far away, we never had a chance to see each other at all. And my daughter was so close to me that I could see her so often. I had no authority to be responsible for my children like I should have, like any other mother would. My soul and my mind were like they had left my body. I felt so emptied. I couldn't say to her, "It's going to be alright honey, I'll get you some salt!". I couldn't promise her anything because I lived under the authority of the Khmer Rouge. Whatever they gave me that is all I got.

The Third Miracle During the day I went to work as usual. That night my daughter didn't come to see me. I returned to work again and discussed it with Souy. After we lined up for our meal we sat inside our mosquito net "mong". She carried her little baby boy to bed. Then she said to me,

"Do not worry too much, Heang. If you think too much you will definitely go insane. Get to bed." It was about five o'clock, and it was still daylight. I was sitting at the bottom of the wooden steps with my feet hung down on the ground. The rain was pouring down really hard. Souy yelled at me, "Heang! Why are you sitting like that? Aren't you afraid to get wet? Come on inside. Can't you see the rain is pouring?" After she said that she went to bed in her mosquito net and I just sat there watching the rain dripping.

      I was hopeless. The rain continued to drop down from the straw used on the roof of the cabin. As I was looking at the straw my eyes were drawn to one drop of rain. My eyes followed that one rain drop from the roof to the ground. The ground began to part with each drop of water. I kept on looking, following each raindrop over and over again, from the roof to the sand that was removed by each raindrop. I stared at it for a while, then I noticed a cork coming out of the ground. I kept on staring and discovered a cork popped up above the ground. I stared until the cork became very clear, then I went down to where it was and parted the soft, sandy wet ground with my fingers. I made sure nobody was looking, especially, Souy. She would definitely think I was crazy for sure. A bottle was buried there, and I tried to pull it up while it was still raining outside. I got excited to find out what was in it. My mind was back in its place. The bottle was filled with very large crystal white salt. The whole pieces of salt were dried inside the bottle. I hid the bottle very quickly. I wrapped my arms around it and brought it upstairs. I was afraid that if Souy found out about this she would never believe it. She would think that I stole it from the cafeteria. So, that's why I hid it from her. This overjoyed me as my daughter had told me how much she wanted to taste salt. I said to myself, "Oh! This is what my daughter wanted. Now, I've got it! Now, I've got this for my daughter."

I never thought that I could do anything to get that because I lived under the communist. But why did I find this salt? My daughter needed and wanted it. I was overjoyed and amazed and wondered again, like when that man handed me the package with the shrimp and honey. That question stuck in my mind. Why did I need this and I've got it, again? I kept wondering and wondering. I was an idolatress, but it never crossed my mind to pray at all. I didn't know why I didn't pray to that god. So, when the miracles happened I never thought of that god helping me. I was just wondering who had done this in my life? I needed this, so why did this thing come as a miracle? Who in the world had buried this? Who made me want to search for it like that? The incident stuck in my head for so long. I received the salt and I was overjoyed. I hid the bottle, not letting Souy find out, because I was guilty of that one thing, when I refused to cooperate with the "Anka" by moving to a different location. So, I refused to get into any more trouble. And if they found out about this, again I would be in trouble for sure. That would make my trial worse and they would accuse me for stealing.

  I would roll some pieces of salt in my handkerchief for my daughter. Whenever she came to sleep with me, I whispered, "Don't let anyone know that you got the salt from me, if you love mom. Do not even ask where I got this from." She said, "Oh! Mother, I won't ask you that. I am so happy as if I received food from heaven!"

  I did that every time she came to see me. My daughter's face lit up ever time I gave her some salt to take with her. She was so happy. Many months past by. The rice planting season had past and we entered the reaping season. When the rice ripened, we didn't know what was going to happen to us. We just waited on the "Anka". Everyone was frightened of the Vietnam soldiers who came into Cambodia to invade the country. Then the leaders of every part of the

Khmer Rouge fled from us. We didn't know where they went. My daughter came to be with me. After she had come I thought about my son. He stayed so far away. All the mothers went to get their sons at that time; they knew all the leaders were escaping from the Vietnamese. They weren't holding us captive. We all went to get our children. One sister came to me and said, "Come on Heang, let us go and get our sons!" Her name was Sister Bahn. And we both went. Some of those children came to their mothers. Those that didn't were afraid. I went with Bahn. We walked along the rice field. When we got there, all the leaders were gone. Only the children were there. We saw them laughing for the first time. They played together as if they had freedom. All the mothers went and got their kids back. They just grabbed their boys by the hands and brought them back.

      When I saw my son, I grabbed his hand, but he shook it off and refused to come with me. He said, "I won't go with you. I'm afraid of the "Anka". If I go with you they will kill me. So, I will not get away from them. I had made a commitment with the "Anka"." He let go of my hand, as if he hated me. I didn't know where he got his saying. I didn't know that he felt that way. I saw all the other children going with their mothers except mine. My only son refused to come with me. He let go of my hand and ran away from me. I cried out loud. I was shaken and my heart was broken, "Why aren't you coming with me? I am your mother?" He said to me, "I will not go, you can go back now." I went back home with the others. They all had their children by the hands smiling at each other. They shared each other's joy. I started to cry out loud. They kept on asking me, "Where is your son?" I cried out, "Oh! Sister, from this point on I will never get to see my son again. I will never see his face again because he has made the commitment with them already. He will not come with me anymore." They all thought I was insane when they saw me crying so loud like that.

They tried to comfort me, "If he loves you he will come to you one of these days for sure. If he doesn't come today, he will come to you another day. Don't get depressed."

We all got to my cottage and my daughter hid herself inside the rolled blanket on my bed. At night she came out. I said, "Oh, honey! When did you get here?" She said, "I came since daylight. I was afraid that somebody might find me and they might take me back, so I hid myself inside your bed," (which was the bed made of the straw). I was delighted to see my daughter there. Since that day on, she stayed with me because her leaders were gone. A few weeks later their leaders had returned, but they did not do any harm to us. They were a little less strict with us. Even the restriction on my visitation of my daughter was a little better than before. I did not know what was going to happen. They said that we all were to move away to another camp.

The Fourth Miracle I was very scared because I was afraid that I would never get to see my son again. Now we're moving away, and I'd never see my son again for the rest of my life. He was falling out of my life. But it was a miracle one day. That very morning as I stepped outside of my cottage, I saw my son laying on the ground. His face was very pale. He looked dead. My daughter and I carried him inside. He was starving to death. His body was so weak. I didn't know how long he went without food. I asked my daughter to go out and steal some rice in the rice field for me to make some rice soup to eat. Sourneat was very small, but she ran quickly and picked some rice and brought it back in the handkerchief. I ground it as if the rice came off the shelves and cooked it in the small teakettle. I fed my son the rice soup. He later got better.

A few weeks later they commanded us to prepare to move to another camp to work. I prepared all my things for the journey. Sister Souy gathered her children together as everyone else did. All her children were together. We let all our children stay in one place as we went and got some straw which the "Anka" gave us to build the roof for another cottage at that new area. After we finished, we could bring our children with us. So, we both carried the straw together. As we got half the way past the field we got to the big public road with much traffic and many cars, which all belonged to the "Anka".

The Fifth Miracle The trucks were carrying all the rice. We didn't know where they were loading them. Everyday they did that. That day it was very humid. I got so tired because of the heat. It was around one or two o'clock in the afternoon. I told Souy, "Sister Souy, I am very tired, it's too hot. Should we rest a little while?" She said, "Oh, Heang, we can find shade under the small "Patrea" tree over there, for the two of us!" We dropped the straw off our shoulders and sat down under the "Patrea" tree. As we were sitting together, Souy said, "Hey, Heang! I think we're going to die very soon." One of our friends had overheard the "Anka" say how they were going to kill the widows very soon. I didn't get discouraged or scared a bit, because death was with me everyday. I answered her, "So, what are we going to do then?" She said, "We've only got one solution. We already have all of our children back together now. So, we ought to flee from this place. Maybe we will be free. If not, we will surely die, because they let us be with our children so they could kill us all together at one time." I then said,"Oh, Sister, where will we go, if they are everywhere, even in places that we don't even know? If we tried to escape we won't get away from their hands." Souy said, "That's alright if we die, at least we tried. As long as we won't stay in one place and let them kill us." I started to think and I told her, "Oh, Sister, I have a brother who had left me for many years, since before the communist came and took over. My brother was a soldier in the Cambodian army. When he started in the military, I lost him. I didn't know whether he was dead or alive. If one day I get to see him again, oh, how happy I would be! I will have someone to depend on. He's a man that would know the way. He would know the places to hide and the quick way to escape from here. If I see him, our journey would be so much easier, so he could lead us." Souy kept asking me about my brother. "How long ago were you separated?" "Since 1975, before the communist invaded our country," I answered. While I was telling her that, I glanced at the big road on the left-hand side. I noticed a person carrying sheaves on each shoulder with one large bag. The weight was overbalanced. He walked as if the loads were very heavy. I said, "Sister Souy, look! Over there in the distant! That's my brother!" That was a very humid day, we were both sweating, it was so hot. We could see the heat and the humidity in the air. As I was telling her, she slapped me, "Heang! Heang! Heang! Oh, poor Heang! You've lost your mind, you're crazy. We were just talking about your brother, how could he be here now? You have to be strong, Heang. Don't you daydream like this. You will definitely be in some kind of depression." I then got very quiet. As that person got a little closer, I said, "The way he walks is definitely my brother." I then stood up. Souy was shocked and she tried to calm me down, "Heang, Heang, I never thought you were in such a bad condition." I yelled very loud, "Brother! Brother Ang!" Then I saw that man drop both bags and stand up listening. I yelled again, "Brother Ang!" Then he ran quickly toward us. Sister Souy couldn't understand why we had just been talking about him and it became reality right away in one moment. She could say I was crazy, but it became reality. As he ran closer and closer, I hugged my brother with joy and compassion. I cried and he cried. Sister Souy was shocked because she thought that I was crazy. She couldn't believe what had just happened. We had just talked about him and he came like that. Then I took my brother, Ang, (Bunna) to see my children. When we returned to our new camp it was raining really hard. We left the straw at the new camp. Then my brother went with me to get my children. We planned to escape but Sister Souy didn't come with us. We fled from there with my older brother, Bunna. We met his wife and her mother. There was a big emergency when many people were on that journey.

This was the third question I carried in my head. I had wondered for a long time why I just thought of my brother and wanted him to be with us to show the way, and he became reality instantly? My brother was separated from us for many years. And why did we meet in just that little moment as I thought about him? This is the fifth question in my life; it made me wonder, who made these things happen? I was amazed. Why, when I thought of him, did he appear? And there wasn't anybody else on that big road, but him. I kept wondering and wondering. I then went to stay with my brother along with my children. He lead me through the journey. The leaders were panicked because they heard that the Vietnamese were coming to Cambodia, so they fled, too.

My brother looked for rice to feed all of us. We had just been freed from the bondage of the "Anka". Everybody else was looking for rice to eat, too, so they were fighting over the rice they found. The rice was left over in the field. We couldn't own anything because the "Anka" took everything from us. After the leaders had fled, we were all set free. We kept on with our journey. When we knew for sure that the Khmer Rouge had left us, my brother took us to our hometown where my parents lived. He left me there and went on with his family. Everybody had returned back to his or her hometown.

I said good-bye to my brother and his family and I went to meet with my mother and older sister, Ouch Houy. We caught a ride along the way. The Vietnamese troop vehicle stopped and they gave us a ride. They couldn't understand us and we couldn't understand them either. They brought us to Battembang. I walked with my children to my mother's house.

It was about eight miles from the city. As we got to my parent's house, I met my mother and she told me that my father had passed away.

In was in deep sorrow. I shaved my hair off out of respect for my father's death. I loved him so much and he loved me, too. I lost my mind because of that loss. My mother would tell me how he wanted to live with me if we ever saw each other again. So, I thought that he was dying because of me, he was grieving over me being away from home for so long.

My mother told me when he died, it was very painless for him. He wasn't sick or anything. One morning, when everybody was ready to go to work, he just laid there in his bed. He just didn't wake up. As she told me all these things, I started to tell my mother about my story. The suffering and the hard time we all went through when we were apart from them. I described to her all the miracles that had happened along the way. Everything that was in my head, I shared with her at that moment. All the questions that were in my mind I shared with her; when we needed the salt, and when we needed the honey, we received the honey. As I waited to see my brother, it was amazing I saw him in a moment. I shared with her the miracles. My mother said, "My daughter, when your father was alive he was so brokenhearted and he thought of you all the time. Your father had told me, "Don't worry about her, this child has a very good angel watching over her. She's not going to die. He kept telling me that." I never thought of it that way, I just questioned all along.

Later, when we lacked everything to survive, we stayed with my older sister Houy. She was married and had a little boy. They took care of my mother all along. We stayed with them since we came back from the communist. I was empty-handed; we had nothing to eat. We were depending on my sister to provide. I felt very uncomfortable. I got very depressed. I didn't know how we were going to survive. What will we do when all the rice we had was gone? How will we survive? People were everywhere since the war was over. I tried to go and search for my husband. I was determined that he was still alive. I thought if he were alive he would look for us or he would've gone to be with his parents.

Many months had passed by and I had never heard from him. That made me want to go and search for him. I thought maybe he went to Thailand. I discussed that with my older brother, Bouy. He had a wife with two children, also. His son, Bae, and his daughter, Sari. And my other older brother, Ang (Bunna) came with us. He was just separated from his wife. He stayed with my sister, too. So, I discussed my plans with my brothers, "If we live here, how are we going to survive? There's just nothing to live on." There wasn't any currency. The most valuable thing we used for money for food was either gold or rice. My mother had kept one pair of my earrings, a bracelet, and my necklace. I traded the earrings and bracelet for rice. I kept the necklace for the future.

I had an idea for leaving my country, my hometown. Both of my brothers agreed to leave with us. They were afraid that the war would happen again and we would surely die. They said that they wanted to go and check out the Thailand border. So, I gave them a pair of my earrings and they went to Thailand to find out what was out there.

When they got back from Thailand, they described the millions of refugees who were on their way toward Thailand. So we packed our things for our journey. They said that the journey didn't seem too rough. I decided to go with them. I got my children and we said good-bye to my mother and my sister and her family. Then, mother decided to go with us, too. She said to my sister, "If she and the kids are leaving, I have to go with them, too. She has no husband and she is still young. I don't trust what's out there." My mother was explaining that to my sister, Houy. Mother came with us. We said good-bye to my sister and her family.

We traveled out of Battembang. There were millions of people on the road. In the woods, my daughter almost stumbled into the land mine; we screamed at her not to step on it. We went across the deep swamp and my mother was so tired. After walking for many days and nights, she said to me, "Go on my daughter, just leave me here. I'm old, I can just die here!" I told her she'd make it, we all would. As we entered Thailand's border there were camps there. The American Red Cross and the Salvation Army people were there to help in the refugee camps. They paid the Thai people to let us stay in that camp and gave us food and clothing. They helped us set up camps for us to live. They built schools and hospitals and set up the habitat program for the school children. They fed us with love and caring. They had showed us their kindness through all that. I couldn't understand why, either. They bought us water. They even built a Buddha Temple and a church nearby for people to choose to worship. They built a home economics school for crafts and arts. I learned how to knit and crochet there. I ran into one of my old friends from Cambodia, Ms. Sophana. She was teaching people how to sew and how to operate the sewing machine. They also had English as a second language school with a little fee.

At that time we got so much peace and we received food everyday. My children were so happy; they had me and they met new friends, they played amongst the other children. We were all well fed. We were so thankful to the American Red Cross. One day a young widow came to me and invited my mother and me to a Bible class at her church. She told me, "We go to learn about Jesus Christ, a Savior." I said to her, "Who is Jesus Christ, why did they claim he is God? Who came to save the world? I already got my own god. My god is in my own nationality. Jesus Christ is an American God. I'm not going to learn that." That lady did not give up on me. She kept asking me to go with her whenever she went. So, one evening, I went along with her. I heard about the salvation of God, Jehovah. That God so loved the world that He gave His only begotten Son, the Lord Jesus Christ to save the world. For all people from all nations.

That caught my attention a little bit. But I still didn't believe. I thought that it was just a fairy tale. Then I returned to my camp. That widow lent me her New Testament Bible. She told me that if I wanted to go with her to learn the Bible at her church, I could go with her every evening. They had Bible Study, they sang praises to the Lord Jesus Christ. I got her Bible and began to read to my mother as a storybook. I couldn't understand at all. The next day I returned her Bible. She invited me to her church again and I went with her. But I still didn't believe. I came home and thought about what we had learned. My question was why did the American people help us? Why had they been so kind to my people? We were two different people, different nationalities, and different faiths. They had all the riches and money in the world, but my country went down, we were so poor. Some of us lost everything, including families. Our country was so small and had been destroyed, but America was so great compared to us. What did they want from us in return? That was the point that got to me, that made wonder. Why did they go through all the trouble in paying Thailand to care for us?

If they hadn't paid the Thai to let us stay in Thailand, we would've been sent back to our country for sure. They had provided us with all kinds of food, supplies, hospitals, schools, etc. They had spent so much on us; why? I had never seen anyone be so kind as those American people. That brought the question into my mind. I kept wondering and wondering.

One day that widow said, "Heang, today there are American missionaries coming to our church. They are going to heal people and share testimonies, give out tracks and Bibles and hymn books for us. Come with me if you'd like. I went with her to find out what was happening. The American pastor taught us, and he put his hands on the sick. They had a Cambodian translator there. He said, "This God is the only one God who is real. Who made the heavens and the earth and everything in it. As I came here I did not depend on myself, but on the Word of the living God. He taught me to do kindness and to do good, to share the gospel with all nations."

That touched my heart and it stayed with me since. I told my mother and then I went to borrow that widow's Bible. I opened the Bible and started to read from the beginning, when God created the heavens and the earth and everything in it. He made the creatures and fish in the sea, etc. As I kept on reading it, I couldn't understand it, but this really got into my heart. When it said, "There's only one God and there's only one universe." I thought to myself, "Buddha never said all these things. He never claimed that he created the heavens and the earth and that he saved us. He never said it. He only taught us how to be a good person, that's all. He never promised that he would come back to save anyone or us from sins. I thought about these things and wondered. As I heard all these words spoken to me, I returned to my camp. I usually shared what I heard with my mother in all aspects.

One day as I was praying, like that lady told me to. I told her that I wanted to believe, but I couldn't believe, what should I do? She said to me, "If you want to believe in Him and you can't, just pray to the Lord and ask Him for help." And I did just that at night. I said in my prayer like this, "Oh Lord Jesus! If you are my true God, please help me believe. I am ignorant and I do not know you. I only heard this through someone else. So, I don't really know whether you are real or not. So, if you are my true God, when you said that you are the God of all nations, please let me believe that you are my God."

I said that prayer every night. I read the Bible because that lady said I could borrow it as long as I wanted to. When I finished, I could return it to her. I just continued to read it. We had nothing else to do there, so I began to read the Bible. They had school for arts and crafts. I took a knitting class. I learned how to knit and crochet there. They opened an English class also, but they charged a small fee. I wanted to go, too, but I was more interested in this new God. I went to that knitting class for free and came home and read the Bible.

My mother listened to me as I read the Bible each night. She didn't believe it either; she was much more interested in the Bible story. She was a strong believer in Buddha. Whatever I heard about Jesus Christ, I shared with my mother. As I was praying, the Lord had been working in my heart. I wanted to read the Bible more and more. I read it again and again everyday. I then decided to give myself to the Lord Jesus Christ. That lady took me with her to get saved with Pastor Halm in Thailand. He was the Cambodian pastor since he was in Cambodia before the war.

I started to give myself to Him and I began to fall in love with the Lord. I wanted to study His words each and every day and I also went to church every day. On that day the pastor taught us from the Bible in the book of John 14:6, "Jesus answered, I am the way and the truth and the life. No one comes to the Father except through me." These words had stayed within my heart. Those words had amazed me, when Jesus said that He is the way, and that no one comes to the Father, but by "Me". I returned home and I shared with my mother everything I had learned. My mind became confused at that moment.

Also, I wanted to learn English and I didn't know what to think. When I went to the craft class to learn how to knit every day and came back home, I read the Bible to my mother. I read from Genesis on ahead. When I got saved they gave me a New Testament Bible, because I didn't know the word of God yet. I took it home with me and as I was reading it, I shared the story in the Bible with my mother. Then I read this beautiful verse in Matthew 6:33, "But seek first his kingdom and his righteousness, and all these things will be given to you as well."

When I was living in the camp with no future or any hope at all, I really didn't know how long we would stay there or whether they'd send us back home or what? I became unsure about what I was going to do there. And I ran into one of my old friends from Cambodia, Sophana. She wasn't a Christian then. She asked me to go and learn how to sew at her school. She was teaching people how to sew for a little fee, but if I went she let me learn it for free. I turned it down; I shared with her about Jesus. When she heard His name, she started to laugh at me. So we left it at that. I started to debate whether or not I should go to English class or go to church to study the whole Bible. But when I read Matthew 6:33 it said it very clearly to me. I should seek first the kingdom of God and everything else will come to pass. I said, "I will give it a try, Lord!"

I wanted to know about God; I could always learn English later according to that scripture. I decided not to learn English. My faith had grown so deep spiritually in the Lord. I knew that I had to learn the Bible at once. I began to grown stronger in faith as I read the Bible from Genesis on, when God created the earth and everything else. Then, all of my life's questions from the past began to dissolve little by little. I was very pleased with the book of Psalms as I read it to my mother each day. I fell in love with the Lord more and more. The Lord had been working in my life. Those things I learned from the Bible had answered all of my life's questions. Those three questions that I had in my mind in all those times. So, I began to tell my mother, "Mother, in this Bible in the book of Matthew 6:33, I found the answer to those questions that I had for so long. Those places where I couldn't understand what the Lord had done, which were the miracles in my life while I was suffering. That is what made me wonder and search for the answer. And now I found Him. Mother, I found the owner of the miracles in my life! He found me first already. He saw my suffering, my bitterness and the pain that I had. And he didn't condemn me while I was a Buddhist. But His grace and mercies are amazing, Mother. Nobody else had done anything like Him.

In Psalm 34:18, He had declared to us, 'The Lord is close to the broken hearted and saves those who are crushed in spirit.' Lord Jehovah is very near to us; to those who are brokenhearted He saved, and those who are crushed in the spirit. "Mother, I found it! This is the verse that did those miracles in my life, which I had been telling you about when we were in Cambodia. When I said, 'I wondered who did that?' I needed the salt, I needed the honey, and I got them all! I wanted to see my brother, I got my brother. And my life, that I was suppose to lose, why did I get free? Why was I different from everyone else? No body could do these things, Mother, only this one true God."

The Lord had seen all of my sufferings and He had chosen me. He chose me since then. But I didn't know it. But He knew my sufferings. He took very good care of me. He saved me from the "valley of the shadow of death". I now love Him more and more, beyond comparison. My mother listened to me but she didn't believe yet. I prayed for her and shared with her everything that I had learned. I read to her daily and she became attached to the Word of God. She still wasn't convinced. I kept on doing the same thing. I took her to church with me all the time. Until one day when I asked her to go to church with me and she gave herself to the Lord Jesus Christ at church. When she returned, she was confused. She asked me, "Daughter, I am very old, how can He love me, for what reason?" I told her, "Mother, it's not because you are ignorant or wise that He took your sufferings. He bled for you, that is amazing enough to know for sure that He loves you. You shouldn't be confused anymore. After you receive Him, nothing should be confused. He loves you not for what you do, but because of who you are."

She became very hungry for the Lord and she started to read the Bible, too, everyday. After church I would read to my children every day. I loved the Lord more and more, as if I was just falling in love for the very first time. At that time my older brother, Ouch Bouy, who was the camp section leader, was in charge of supplies, such as food. When he saw me and my mother and the children receive Jesus Christ as our Personal Savior, he became very angry and my other brother, Ouch Bunna or Ang, met a woman and he left us. We lived near my brother, Bouy. He was very annoyed and very disturbed at me every day. He made his five year old boy, Bae, mock Christians. He saw us praising the name of Jesus with songs and became angrier with us. He said we came to this place and we were so ignorant that we began to accept a foreign God, who belongs to American people; he wasn't friendly with us since.

We were so filled with joy and the Holy Spirit was upon us. Each day we were hungry for His Words. One day my brother mocked the name of the Lord as he gave us the food. He used to call us to pick them up, now he just ignored us and told his children not to bother us and said, "Don't you let them know that their food is here, let that Jesus come and receive it Himself." As I heard that I told Sourneat to go and get the food. I received all of his angry words, but they didn't bother me at all. We were too happy for anything like that to bring us down.

I was so overjoyed with the Lord to be discouraged. Nobody can take those feelings away from me. A few months later he decided to return to Cambodia. Before that everybody in that camp begged him and his family to stay. Everybody gathered their life histories and put them in the application requesting to be sponsored to come to the United States of America and Australia and France. I had no hope in going to either place because we had no one there. Other families had families in foreign countries to sponsor them. I never thought of that. I just thought of the joy to know the Lord Jesus Christ. We just learned the Bible. We enjoyed all the pastors coming and going out of our church. American pastors went there every day. I was so happy beyond any comparison in listening to His wonderful words. Every secret in His words has now been revealed into my heart. I didn't really worry about whether we could come to these countries at all. At that time everyone was getting their applications filled to seek sponsorships from other countries.

    One day a lady came to me and said, "Heang, if you want to apply to come to America or France or Australia, you can. I will bring you an application to fill out. I filled that application with information on my family; my husband was deceased serving the war for the Regime of Lon Nol. But I didn't expect to come to America. That didn't worry me a bit because I was so happy in studying the Word of God. Until one day I heard that my brother Ouch Bouy and his family decided to return back to Cambodia. I was wondering, "What made them want to go back?" We came to this place because we already knew what it was like back there. For what reason did they go back there? Why didn't he fill out an application to come to America like everyone else? The Lord prepared for us to come, in case we would get it, even if we didn't know anyone in America. But he didn't listen to me, he was too mad at all of us. He got his wife and two children and returned back home. I felt so sorry for the kid's future. At that time nothing made me happier than studying the Word of God every day. And I understood that word and I wanted to share the gospel with any stranger. I wasn't any type of theologian, but I understood His Word so deep, the Holy Spirit touched my heart. When I saw the elderly lady who lived next door to us, I went to see her and said, "Um (which means uncle or aunt in a respectful way of speaking to the elderly, I wanted to read to you a beautiful story from the Bible. Would you like to hear me reading it to you? She said, " I do not believe in Jesus Christ; I don't want to hear about Him."

I didn't give up on that. I said to her the next time, "Um, I want to read you this story". What story?" she asked. I started to read to her the book of Daniel. Every day as I was reading to her and her friend, they became very interested in the story at first and then they believed in the Word of God. The woman later gave her life to the Lord Jesus Christ. I give all the glory and honor to the Lord Almighty. A few months later someone in camp ran and told me that they saw my name on the bulletin board to come to America. We got so excited that we got the chance to come, I knew God's hands are so big for me. I had filled out applications to go to Australia, France, and America. The Lord had opened the way for us all to come to America, because He knew that this was the best place for us.

In the fall of 1981 we came to Pennsylvania, USA. We learned everything from television and from people around us at church and from neighbors. The Lord had provided every need more abundantly.

My life and my mother's life and my kid's lives were changed completely. When we were walking through Thailand my mother didn't think she was able to make it. She was in her fifties then. She didn't think she could make it through the journey. She told me to leave her there in the jungle, because she thought that she was going to die. I carried my mother through the journey. She now is still living happily in the Lord in California. She has been back to Cambodia to visit her children and grandchildren about five times now. She came to visit us two times. She's now eighty years old and she still loves the Lord, praise be the Name of the Lord.

When we got to America my mother continued to pray for my brother, Ouch Bouy who went back home because he hated Jesus. She continued to minister to him through letters and with missionaries who went down there. We sent him a Bible and money along with the tapes of the gospels and tracks. My brother was very rebellious with the Lord. One day he got shot in one of his legs and he had to get it amputated. While he was lying there in the hospital bed, he had nothing. Both of his children had to drop out of school to support the family. He had no money to pay for the hospital bills. God had laid a burden on my heart and I sent money to him without even knowing about his situation. My brother read my mother's letter and he heard tapes of the gospel of Jesus Christ. The next time they went to Cambodia my brother cried so deep and he got saved. He found the Lord Jesus Christ when he received His Words through my mother's letters and tapes and through missionaries. When he received the money that we sent to him, it was just enough to cover the hospital bills. He cried out and he knew he was wrong when he returned, just because he was mad at us for being Christians. He had hardened his heart to not except the truth from God's plan in his life and his family. Now, he found the Lord's mercies upon him. He gave himself to the Lord. And now he is a very humble pastor in the "Undongpreng Village". Now, all of my family is saved!

I give thanks to the Lord Jesus Christ for saving my soul

and for dying for my sins because I was a sinner and lived in darkness. When I worshiped the false god, Buddha, who could not hear or see me when I prayed. I thank the Lord for touching the American Red Cross people to come and help us in Thailand. I give my thanks to the Lord for saving my life and for His mercies that endure forever.

When I looked back into my life story, I could never live without Jesus. And He chose me, since I was living in darkness and did not know Him. But His light has brought me here. His mercies are incredible for such a person as I. He loves me and He loves you. That is a joy to my soul to know that. Psalm 139 declares that He knew my entire secret place in my heart. He knows all of my sufferings and all of my needs. Nothing can hide you or me from His presence. He is alive! Praise God for that. He is so wonderful and He met every need even to this day.

If you read my testimony and you feel the Lord leading you to believe in Him, just accept that gift of life now. Accept the Lord as your personal Savior and you shall be saved. If you just believe that He is the Son of God and confess that through your mouth and believe in your heart, you shall be saved. My friend, there is no other way but through our Lord Jesus Christ; just repeat this prayer,

"Lord Jesus, I know that I am a sinner. Please forgive me. I believe that Jesus Christ is the Son of God, that He died for my sins and God, the Father, raised Him from the dead. I now accept the Lord Jesus Christ as my Lord and Savior. Please, Lord Jesus, come into my heart. Amen!"

After you say this prayer and believe in your heart, you shall be saved. When I worshiped Buddha, it was my religion, but when I received Jesus Christ, it is a relationship. The religion was because man made the god, but a relationship with the Lord Jesus Christ is with the One who created humans and the world. And He is alive! With power and might and authority. Everything is in Him, treasure, love, relationship, success, wisdom, etc. If you want all those things you must go through Him. He will always provide all of your needs and mine. He will always give you more than what you could even think of to ask from Him. He is faithful and just to forgive us from all sins and cleanse us from all unrighteousness, as 1 John 1:9 declared, *If we confess our sins, he is faithful and just to forgive us our sins, and to cleanse us from all unrighteousness. If we say that we have not sinned, we make him a liar, and his word is not in us.*

He doesn't just save your soul, but He will do all the things that you need from Him. My beloved, God chose me since I had nothing but one pair of clothes. Now, I've got so much more; more than enough is God's blessing to His children. It's because of His mercies that He is faithful to all of us, even when we don't deserve it, but just don't ignore His presence. If He did these things for me, He will do it for you; so much more beyond what you could imagine. As the book of Philippians 4:19 said, *And my God shall supply all your need according to His riches in glory by Christ Jesus.*

I can't live without the Lord Jesus Christ. And today my God is still doing these things in my life. He gives me great miracles, because He is alive. He didn't do these things because I'm good, no, but because of His mercies on me. And I can still see everything that happened to me in my life every time. I often share these things with my two children. We are still amazed at all the blessings that He is still doing in our lives.

Every trial and testing, He made us whole again through faith. Every time I think I can see the Lord in it. He is real to my life and He is patient. Friend, you have just made the most important decision of your entire life and have entered from death into life eternal.

    I learned to trust in Him, when good or bad things happened, I just trusted Him and gave Him all of the glory and praise. His mercies are always with me. He is my everything in my life. I can't breathe without Him. Please read the Bible; that's how I came to know Him. The more I read of Him, the more closely I walk with Him and I love it. I promise you, the more you know Him personally the more you're going to love Him. Thank you for your mercy my sweet Lord Jesus, I know that I am a sinner but I'm free because of you.

Heang O. Horm

PART III

"GOD DID IT"

The story of ten years of the faithfulness of the Lord at Immanuel Baptist Church, in Richmond, Virginia

By Pastor W. E. Sampson

"The Lord hath done great things for us; whereof we are glad."
Psalm 126:3

PREFACE

On September 17th, 1944, we celebrate the occasion of the Tenth Anniversary of our ministry at Immanuel Baptist Church, Richmond, Va. They have been ten years of precious memory in our own life, and I am sure there are hundreds who have, through these years, been richly blessed of the Lord. It is after some prayer and thoughtful consideration of the guidance of the Lord, that I undertake to write this little book which is a testimony to the leading of the Lord during these ten years. It came to me all of a sudden that this was the work of the Lord, and because God really did all that was done, that the name of the book should be "GOD DID IT". Because it was God, indeed, who did it. We set forth everything you read in these pages, as a testimony to His glory, and dedicate the book to the one who means everything to me, Jesus Christ, my Saviour and Lord.

W. E. Sampson,
Richmond, Va.

Chapter I

"Behold, I have set before thee an open door, and no man can shut it." Revelation 3:8

Men often take themselves very seriously in matters which are quite trivial. This is so often true in work for our Lord. It is not in a sense of superficial humility that I open this presentation this way. I really mean it from my heart when I say that the work of the past ten years at the Immanuel Baptist Church in Richmond, Virginia, was not my doing, but the Lord's.

God uses men, but the men God uses are nothing more than common clay in His hands. To no man should credit go for the slightest success in God's vineyard. Paul may plant and Apollos water, but it is God alone who can give the increase. So when you review the ten years from September 17th, 1934, to September 17th, 1944, just say "God did it". He opened the door, has kept it open, and will keep it open until He sees fit to shut it.

You and I have been the tools for His hand. Do not, therefore, boast of anybody's work but His. He did it.

It was in the summer of 1934 that we first heard of Immanuel Baptist Church and the first circumstances were rather peculiar. At the time, we were pastoring a church in Illinois, where the Lord was blessing. Souls were being saved there. Our young folk were answering the call to Christian service. We were very happy in our work.

That summer, we were asked to conduct a "revival meeting" at a church in Chesterfield County, Virginia. Our kinsfolk lived in Richmond, and we were able to visit with them and conduct this series of meetings at the same time. This was the usual way we spent our "vacation", in soul winning missions. So that summer found us "resting" in Virginia.

One day during that series of meetings, a lady who was interested in the work of the country church told me of the visit of one of the deacons of Immanuel Baptist Church to their home. She said that a group of the folk from there was coming out to the meetings one night. Sure enough they came. Among the group were some men and women I had known in former days in Richmond, and I was delighted to meet them again. After the meeting that night they asked me if I could preach for them one Sunday before returning to Illinois. I was unable to do so. They pressed the invitation and finally I agreed to lead prayer meeting on the Wednesday night before returning to my work out west. I can well remember preaching on the subject, "A VISION FROM GOD", and I preached almost an hour, something I seldom do. After the meeting that night the deacons asked me to meet with them, and I enjoyed an hour or so with them. I say enjoyed, well the fellowship was a joy. What they talked to me about were their troubles. They were in debt. They were discouraged. They didn't see any way out for their church. There were less than a hundred people supporting the work. From a financial point of view they were bankrupt. Humanly speaking, the whole thing seemed impossible. Humanly speaking, yes, but with God "all things are possible". They told me about their debts. There was a building debt mounting so high that they could not curtail the principal, and interest was going unpaid. There was a large amount due the pastor. There was a note in this bank, and another note at that bank. Then there was the coal bill far past due, and winter was coming again. Yes, they had tried to get a pastor, but they couldn't pay enough to interest the man who could do the job right. So there they were. The supply pastor had written to the seminary and described this dilemma and suggested that they might pay a young man $50.00 per month, but the seminary had responded that they didn't have a man who could fit the job. Yet, here was an opportunity for someone who would really seek to do God's work. What these people needed was encouragement.

I advised them not to meet together and bemoan their inability to get a preacher, but to take it to the Lord in prayer, and ask God for a man. I am told they did this. My call to this pastorate came after this plan was followed. I do praise the Lord that I am pastor of Immanuel Baptist Church as a result of prayer. That is the way God does. He puts it on the hearts of people to come to Him in their desperation. Then he answers their prayer.

It might be interesting to some of our present members and friends who didn't know about those days at Immanuel, to read the letter that came to me as the "call" to the church. Here it is word for word:

Dear Brother Sampson:

Confirming our telegram of yesterday, we beg to advise that our pulpit committee was appointed on August 12th, which met on that day to consider calling a pastor, and after careful and prayerful consideration, the committee present were ready to extend the call at that time, but thought it wise to have another meeting to pray over the matter. We met the second time on August 15th and the committee unanimously agreed to recommend to the church that you be invited to become our Pastor, and the committee's recommendation was unanimously adopted by the church in business session at the close of the morning service on yesterday.

The church debts and obligations are as follows:

Church mortgage	$17,500.00
Baptist Council	1,400.00
Former Pastor	300.00
Church note	375.00
Church note (Int. Borrowed)	740.00
Some current debts	125.00

The current interest on our church mortgage is $262.50 every three months.

Brother Kirk says turn in your Bible, 3rd chapter of Acts, 6th verse, and you will have our sentiments in this matter. May the Lord direct you in answering our call for help as He did Paul in the call to the Macedonians.

Our prayers are following you in all of your future activities.

With warm Christian love to you, Mrs. Sampson and son.

Yours in His service,
PULPIT COMMITTEE,
Immanuel Baptist Church.

This letter presented the financial condition rather correctly. Perhaps a few more bills could have been added, as the total debts actually were about $22,000.00 when we went over them in our first meeting on finances.

"But why did you come?" you ask.

"Was it because it offered a big salary?"

Well surely Acts 3:6 is not an offer of a big salary. Did you read it?

"Was it because if offered a 'promotion' in the ministry?"

Surely if you could have seen the church then and the one in Illinois you wouldn't say so.

"Then why did you come?" you insist.

There is but one answer to that question, and only one. It was the call of God. When God calls, it is not for us to say what we want to do. We answer His call and go where He says go. We answered God's call, and we came. The way He led and supplied the need for our move is a story all by itself. Suffice it to say that in it all, He left no doubt as to what His will was for us.

Indeed He opened a door. He said, "This is the door, go through." What else could I do? Was I not His servant? Had I not said to Him that I would go where He wanted me to go, and that I'd do what He wanted me to do? Well, He said to me, "Go to Richmond." I went. Well, here I am.

****

A father in the armed service, saved a year and a half ago, says: "I praise the Lord for my deliverance from sin, being washed by the precious blood of my Saviour, through the preaching of the Word at Immanuel Church, used by the Holy Spirit to bring it about."

Another father who was saved seven years ago writes: "One night I caught a glimpse of Calvary as you preached and I walked up the aisle as "Just As I Am" was being sung, and surrendered to Christ. Hallelujah!"

A mother who had been saved twenty-five years, dedicated her life to the Lord during these years and writes: "I did not have assurance of my salvation until I started going to Immanuel Church. I learned, also, the importance of living a testimony of showing forth Christ each day and having a separated life. But praise God, I know now!"

A lady who consecrated her heart and life to the Lord during this past ten years writes: "The Bible teaching at Immanuel has made me love God's Word and enjoy reading it. The emphasis on soul winning has made me yield myself to the Lord to give out this glorious gospel, and the emphasis on missions has given me a greater passion for the lost on foreign fields!"

CHAPTER II

"I have begun to give ....begin to possess."   *Deuteronomy 2:31*

Yes, God did it. He opened the door that could not be shut except by His own hand. Now He starts to give, and day by day for ten years He has given, and all that we had to do was to possess the blessings. The only need we have felt along the way has been our need of Him constantly. The promise of Joshua 1:9 has been ours, "The Lord thy God is with thee." Even as Joshua needed the hand of the Lord with him, facing the conquest of Canaan, so we have felt the need of the hand of the Lord with us as we have sought the conquest of "Immanuel". Those years are now written into the pages of history. The history of Immanuel is truly HIS-story, for it is an account of His work.

Yes, from the beginning He has been with us. Through the ten years we have been forced to stay before the Lord in prayer. God has assured us that He was with us. What there was of foundation had been well nigh shaken from beneath the structure of the church's morale. Surely there was a great problem of putting foundation walls under a tottering structure. It meant God had to be with us. There were only a handful of us–about a hundred or less the first Sunday. I remember there were one hundred and ten in Sunday school. Soon, the attendance was increasing. It reached over a hundred, then a hundred and fifty and then on and on, until today the church that seats nearly five hundred is usually well filled, and sometimes on special occasions is overcrowded. It is not to our glory, but to the glory of our Lord Jesus Christ that it has been done.

We do not want to overemphasize the financial, but there is no way we can give God the glory for the way this work has progressed, if we fail to give the praise due Him for leading forth in this part of the work.

It might be of some interest to look at a report of the Treasurer ten years ago. Our first full month was the month of October, 1934. The collections reported were as follows:

October 7th $50.59
October 14th 53.13
October 21st 58.25
October 28th 58.75

Somebody with a very generous heart gave $50.00 to the Treasurer, and somebody else interested in getting some song books contributed $10.00 for that purpose. Added up, the total collections for the month totaled $280.72.

That was back at the beginning. The Lord was precious to us in the way He supplied them. It has continued through the years. Not one promise of the Lord has failed. In 1943, the last full year's report from our Treasurer, the gifts averaged $530.00 per week for the whole year. That is ten times the average weekly offering of ten years ago. Brethren, this is not the work of men, but the work of God. This is God's answer in material things. This is His response to meet all needs when we do what He says, and are faithful in giving forth the Word of life.

In the beginning there was a sad lack of missionary zeal. Yes, there was the usual W. M. U., but there can be a W. M. U. without a zeal for missions. Two hundred and seventy-four dollars was the total missionary giving that year, and that money had been diverted to help pay the interest on our mortgage.

In the beginning, there were names on the roll, but just a few were actually standing by the work. There were five hundred and eighty-eight names on the roll, and one of our Deacons on many occasions would say, "I felt like those 588 members were 588 stones tied around my neck." It is doubtful if we have as many names on the roll today. However, the roll we have today is not just a list of names, but members indeed. We have kept both doors open, the front door and the back. God has blessed the use of both. We have witnessed God's blessing on our effort to keep the church clean. Such only are vessels unto honor.

In the beginning, we had an auditorium that was dirty and dingy for lack of care, and of all colors—blue! That first year we started to paint it. Pastor, deacons and others gave of their time, and we painted it. You wouldn't know the place. What a transformation! All it takes is a little paint.

In the beginning, we needed a spiritual revival. Oh, how we needed it. How our city needed it. How we prayed for it. A real awakening did come, and we praise the Lord for it. We pray God that every one of our people will dedicate themselves anew to a life of prayer and devotion to the end that the fire that started here ten years ago will never dim—but burn on and on to the glory of God.

In the beginning, we needed men and women, and young folk. We needed everything. God put His hand on this work, and He gave us what we needed.

For ten years now, God has given. He has been continually on the giving hand. He began to give, and He has never stopped giving. It has been to the extent to which we have possessed His gifts that we have shared the blessedness of it all.

Perhaps we ought to meditate more on this great truth. He gave and still gives. Are you enjoying the blessedness of God that goes with possessing the blessings given?

Chapter III

"Preach the Word,...reprove, rebuke, exhort with all longsuffering and doctrine." II Timothy 4:2

Principles never change. It was on this premise that we preached a message on the night of January 2nd, 1938, entitled "His Testimony". That message was a blessing to many, and so mightily did God use it that it was thought well to print it. Because of the spiritual blessing it was to many, we are reprinting it here in abridged from. We trust you will read it with much prayer and be thrilled again at its content:

"HIS TESTIMONY"

"He that hath received His testimony hath set to his seal that God is true." John 3:33

"His Testimony!" What a great relief it is to be able to say that Immanuel Church is His testimony, the testimony of Christ. No, not the testimony of a man, or an organization, or of some program, but His testimony, the testimony of Jesus Christ the Lord. The testimony of what He has done, is doing and will yet do in the hearts and lives of them that know Him as their Saviour and have made Him the Lord of their lives.

This message is not being given in the spirit of boasting. "God forbid that I should glory save in the cross of our Lord Jesus Christ, by whom the world is crucified unto me, and I unto the world." (Gal. 6:14) We do not feel that Immanuel Baptist Church is any better than any other church, but we do want this church to be wholly dedicated to the Gospel of our Lord and Saviour, Jesus Christ, and if every church in the world falls into the apostasy that is gaining such headway in these days, we hope and pray that the Lord may keep this testimony true to Himself.

I have a feeling that this is His testimony because of the way it has been built. It can be truly said of the Immanuel Baptist Church that it died and rose again from the dead. The resurrection of this church from the dead is one of the miracles of recent years. I do not mean that it was a miracle that the church came back from a terrible crisis, but the miracle was the way it came back.

It did not rise from the dead in the conventional way. Like Lazarus, it came forth at the call of the Lord, and it had to be unwound from its grave clothes, and the marvel of its testimony has been the means of many believing on the Lord Jesus Christ.

I. "His Testimony" here is one that magnifies the truth and inspiration of the whole Word of God.

We are living in days when men are putting question marks on the Bible. We believe "all scripture is given by inspiration of God and is profitable for doctrine, for reproof, for correction, for instruction in righteousness." (II Tim. 3:16) We believe that "holy men of God spake as they were moved by the Holy Ghost." (II Peter 1:21)

We make no apology for our belief in the verbal and plenary inspiration of the Word of God, and when we say that, we include the Old as well as the New Testament. We take the whole book as the Word of God and believe everything written in it, whether we can understand it or not.

In our preaching service, in our prayer gatherings, in our Bible School on Sunday morning, and in our Training Unions, the Bible has been the text book, and a knowledge of what the Book says has been the groundwork. We have found that a spiritual growth has come wherever quarterlies, magazines and other helps have been supplanted by the Word of God itself. We do not mean to say that we ignore what anyone else has to say, but we do mean to say that we take God's Word first, and what others have to say is, comparatively speaking, a passing moment in the matter.

It has also been necessary, because of our conviction that "His Testimony" must be built on "His Word", that whenever we have come face to face with programs that were not in conformity to "His Word", that we could not work together with them because "His Testimony" required loyalty to "His Word." If we have been criticized for this, we are sorry. "His Word" and loyalty to it are more important than the approval of men.

It is our belief that we are not only expected to believe God and His Word, but to do what He says. Therefore, whatsoever is written in the Word in principle or action for a Christian is applicable to each member of this church. Loyalty to His Word is not only to believe what it says about what we ought to do, but to do it as well.

We believe, too, that when His Word says that we are not to receive or give Godspeed to one who denies the Word, that it is the Christian's duty to follow the Word of God implicitly, and this we do. (Read II John 7-11)

If this is being peculiar, being different, being non-cooperative, then that's not our fault. We are under bond to be true to God, and if being true to God and His Word puts us in discord with the powers that be, then we will have to be in discord with the powers that be.

We read in the Holy Word that the "Word of God is quick, and powerful, and sharper than any two-edged sword, piercing even to the dividing asunder of soul and spirit, and of the joints and marrow, and is a discerner (lit. critic) of the thoughts and intents of the heart." (Heb. 4:12) It is our earnest hope that through the intensive study and proclamation of the naked Word of God, that men and women will thus be convicted and turn to the Christ of Calvary as their Saviour. We are under definite marching orders from above to preach it without fear or favor.

II. "His Testimony" here is one that magnifies the threefold ministry of Christ: He came to offer Himself as a Sacrifice for men's sins: He is now our interceding Advocate and Intercessor, and He is coming again as our Glorious Lord to reign.

"His Testimony" here demands that we preach these truths without one ounce of compromise.

a. "He died for our sins according to the scriptures." (I Corinthians 15:3)

"Be not thou therefore ashamed of the testimony of our Lord...who hath saved us, and called us unto an holy calling, not according to our works, but according to His own purpose and grace, which was given us in Christ Jesus." (II Tim. 1:8-9)

How marvelously the Gospel truth of redemption through the blood is taught in the whole Word of God.

"For I am not ashamed of the Gospel of Christ; for it is the power of God unto salvation to everyone that believeth." (Rom. 1:16)

If there are any that do not like this kind of testimony, all we want to say is that this is the message of God's Word.

We do not acclaim church membership. We believe everyone who accepts Christ as his Saviour and wants to make Him Lord of his life, should come into fellowship with a church where the Gospel is taught, and the flock fed on the Word of God. But church membership never saves a soul.

We do not acclaim water baptism. We believe in it, and insist that everyone who is born again should be baptized according to the command of the Lord. But baptism can never give a lost sinner a new life.

We do not acclaim morality. We believe in clean living, and especially insist that every believer should "live soberly, Godly and righteously in this present life." But no amount of morality can get a man inside the portals of glory.

We believe in the power of God to save men from sin, because "all have sinned" and all need a Saviour and "there is none other name under heaven given among men whereby we must be saved" except the name of Jesus Christ, God's only begotten Son.

We do not preach acceptance of Christ plus these other things, but salvation through the blood of Christ, by grace, through faith, plus nothing. Salvation is not of works lest any man should boast. In God's plan of salvation, the merit of salvation is in the person of the Son who died at Calvary, and the plea of every lost sinner is the blood of the Lamb of God spilled at Golgotha.

Christ is the One who saves; it is the blood that pays the redemption price; it is His provided righteousness that justifies. It is faith in Him and His work that brings the sinner into saving relationship with God.

b. "If any man sin (any believer) we have an advocate with the Father; Jesus Christ the righteous." (I John 2:1)

Christ now is seated at the right hand of God the Father on high. There He sits today as my Advocate to plead the cause for this poor sinner saved by grace. He sits there, the Man in glory, between a Holy God and a poor sinner. If it were not for Him there, what a sad plight mine would be indeed, and yours, too. But praise God, the Word of God says He is there. I believe implicitly, and this church teaches without wavering, that our God-man is there, and what a security it is for us to know that with Him there we are secure from the ravages and attacks and accusations of Satan.

c. "Looking for that blessed hope and glorious appearing of the great God and our Saviour Jesus Christ."

Praise God, the Bible teaches that the same Lord of Glory is coming again. There are some who think we are fanatical when we say we believe Christ is coming again, but I say, dear friends, that the Bible teaches that He is coming again. (I Thes. 4:15-18) He is coming again, and the coming is the thing that will set the world right again. The world is not getting better, but according to the Word of God "evil men will wax worse and worse". (II Timothy 3:13) According to the Word, "In the last days perilous times shall come. (II Timothy 3:1-7) Apostasy is the trend of the church and such is prophesied in the Word.

When the cup of iniquity shall run full, Christ is coming (II Thes. 1:7-10). We believe and teach these great Bible truths.

Salvation is three fold: At Calvary He died for us; now He lives on high for us and in the person of the Holy Spirit is in us; and He is coming again for us.

When He died for us He met the PENALTY for the guilt of our sin; now He provides for salvation from the POWER of sin; and when He comes again He will save us from the very PRESENCE of sin.

III. "His Testimony" here is one that magnifies salvation through Christ and Christ alone.

There are those who are guilty of saying that there is one Heaven, and many roads thereto. That is not so. The Bible says "there is none other name under heaven given among men whereby we must be saved". (Acts 4:12) There is not a Baptist way, a Methodist way, a Presbyterian way, and a Catholic way. There is but one way—The Bible Way.

It is clearly taught in the Bible that all men need to be

saved. "Except a man be born again, he cannot see the kingdom of God." (John 3:3) "For all have sinned and come short of the glory of God." (Romans 3:23) "We are all as an unclean thing, and all our righteousnesses are as filthy rags." (Isaiah 64:6) "All we like sheep have gone astray; we have turned everyone to his own way." (Isaiah 53:6)

It is clearly taught in the Word of God that no man is capable of saving himself, for "not by works of righteousness which we have done, but according to His mercy He saved us." (Titus 3:5) "By the works of the law shall no flesh be justified." (Gal. 2:16) "There is a way which seemeth right unto a man, but the end thereof are the ways of death." (Prov. 14:12) "Jesus said...I am the way, the truth, and the life; no man cometh unto the Father but by me." (John 14:6)

Again the Word proclaims that because of the provision already made, no man can provide for his own salvation. Jesus "in His own body on the tree" bore our sins as is plainly recorded in I Peter 2:24. "For Christ also hath once suffered for sins, the just (righteous) for the unjust (unrighteous), that He might bring us to God." (I Peter 3:18) According to II Corinthians 5:21, Jesus, who knew no sin, became sin for me that I might become the righteousness of God in Him. "For God so loved the world that He gave His only begotten son, that whosoever believeth in Him should not perish, but have everlasting life." (John 3:16)

And what does the sinner have to do to save himself? Absolutely nothing. He just turns from the old life of sin to Christ by faith in all He has done for the poor sinner, and the poor sinner becomes a saved sinner. "Believe on the Lord Jesus Christ and thou shalt be saved." (Acts 16:31)

This plan of salvation is "His Testimony", and with the help of God we will make it the appeal of "His Testimony" at old Immanuel.

IV. "His Testimony" here is one that magnifies the Holy Spirit of God as the one who accomplishes things for the Lord.

The church of today has not lost its preachers, but its power. Power with God is because of the presence and filling of the Holy Spirit. The Holy Spirit is not just a phantom idea. He is a person.

He is a power-giving person. If we are to see the working of the power of God, there must be a return to power of the Holy Ghost in the heart and life of the believer and the church.

The Holy Spirit convicts of sin, of righteousness and of judgement. If we preach the Word in the power and unction of the Holy Spirit, then souls must be saved. (John 16:8-11)

The Holy Spirit indwells, sanctifies, directs, teaches and fills the surrendered Christian and uses, in His service, the born again child of God, who will let Him have His way with him.

Jesus said when the Holy Spirit was come, He would "testify of me." (John 15:26) When the Lord ascended on high, He sent the Holy Spirit, who filled the believers at Pentecost. (Acts 2)

The Holy Spirit was the guiding genius of the first century church. The preaching of the apostolic days was preaching in Holy Spirit power. (1 Cor. 2:1-5)

We believe in a personal Holy Spirit at Immanuel Church, and will continue to depend on Him to do His work.

V. "His Testimony" here magnifies the need of a depth of consecration and a real separation from the world.

At this point we have heard repercussions and explosions. God demands surrender and separation on the part of His people, and the only person who can rightly expect God's blessing on their service and life, is the one who has laid their all on the altar and has come out of the world and intends to live a separated life for the Lord.

"I beseech you therefore, brethren, by the mercies of God, that ye present your bodies a living sacrifice, holy, acceptable unto God, which is your reasonable service. And be not conformed to this world, but be ye transformed by the renewing of your mind, that ye may prove what is that good, and acceptable, and perfect, will of God." (Romans 12:1-2)

"Wherefore, come out from among them, and be ye separate, saith the Lord." (II Cor 6:17)

The tragedy of the testimony of Christendom today is that it is compromising, worldly, ungodly, and tainted with the filth of this world.

At Immanuel, we hope, by the help of the Holy Spirit, to seek out the "filth of the leaven of this world" and put it outside our testimony. We recognize the fact that we cannot govern the personal habits of our members, but we are also happy that a large group of our people have come to see that a testimony that will honor God cannot partake of the filthy habits of this world, that harm our bodies "which are temples of the Holy Ghost", and that the surrendered life is the one that God can use. (Romans 6:11-17)

To this doctrine and practice our ministry is dedicated. "His Testimony" at Immanuel Church may not be perfect, but it will not tolerate any teaching that does not make for holy living.

VI. "His Testimony" here has been one that magnifies the ability of the Lord to meet every material need, and demands of us to use His plan and program in the operation of it.

Hudson Taylor said, "God's work, done in God's way, will never lack for God's supply."

The matter of how to operate the work that bears the name of the Lord is important; because if it is operated according to His will and way, then we can expect His approval and support, materially as well as spiritually.

Has not God said that "whatsoever we ask in the name of the Lord Jesus" shall be done? And are we not told to "seek first the kingdom of God and His righteousness, and all these things shall be added unto us?"

When I first started out in the pastorate, I felt there was a great need for Christian men and women to trust the Lord. I felt it so strongly that I said within myself, "Why doesn't somebody try God's way of financing a church?" When I began to investigate, I found there were some. In every instance where God's method was employed, they were enjoying not only success materially, but spiritual blessings that were not present in those institutions where extraneous methods were in vogue.

God's plan of financing a church is not by devising methods. Oyster suppers, bazaars, shows, soup sales, pledges, every member canvasses and the like, might be all right from man's point of view, but when I studied my Bible I found that the simple Bible way was in every respect sufficient.

The Bible way was:
a. On the first day of the week to lay by in store. (I Corinthians 16:2)
b. Giving was to be "as God has prospered them"; that meant proportionately. (I Corinthians 16:2)
c. Liberality in giving, and not sparingly, is commended of God. (II Corinthians 9:6)
d. God loves a cheerful giver, therefore let men give as they purpose in their hearts. (II Corinthians 9:7)
e. Giving is a grace, and God is able to make that grace abound in men's lives, just as he makes other graces abound. (II Corinthians 9:8)

There is no man-made method here. There is no suggestion of sitting down and urging a person to put down a pledge on the dotted line. We are not saying that it is a sin to make a pledge, but we have found that the free-will way without pressure makes for a better spiritual life in the church, and it does accomplish the result. Furthermore, that's God way.

But there is more than one side to this financial program of the Lord's Testimony. We must be just as careful with the outgo of it as we are with the income of it.

It would be tragic to ask God's people to pray about giving; see them give, and them proceed to use a man-made method in disposing of it. Money given to this church is God's money. To waste one penny of it is to waste God's money. What right have I, as a servant of God, to waste His money? Therefore, we keep the local expenditures to the very minimum.

Neither do we waste money entrusted to us for missionary purposes. We will not pass an entrusted fund into the hands of a board or secretary, where we know a large amount of it will be deducted for salaries and overheads at home, when we know that it can be sent without that deduction, directly to the field. For that reason our church has found that it cannot support so-called "co-operative" campaigns that include heavy home expenditures like military schools, modernist colleges, dead theological seminaries and hospitals with infidel doctors. Whenever a person puts money into our treasury with the desire to use it to the glory of the Lord in foreign fields, we send it to missionaries; they believe the whole Word of God and give their time to spreading the Gospel without thought of salary. They give every ounce of their life's blood for nothing more than daily bread and raiment.

Certainly, no thinking person could condemn that policy concerning finances, and these years of experience prove that it works.

With oyster suppers, stews, bazaars and hen parties–plus big super million-dollar campaigns for missions on man's methods, we were headed for the rocks –financially.

With God's method in "His Testimony" in three years, the income of the church has more than doubled. They can give this poor preacher "down the country" wherever they go, but it will take a lot of rubbing to erase the proof in black and white, that proves "My God shall supply all your need according to His riches in glory by Christ Jesus." (Philippians 4:19)

VII. If "His Testimony" here continues, it must magnify the great commission. Christ Jesus left the parting words to the Disciples, "Go ye therefore, and teach all nations." (Matthew 28:19)

What a task there is before us. "His Testimony" here has a challenge. In the first century, the church took the commission literally. They went out to tell a world lost in sin, that Jesus Christ, who had been crucified, died, buried and risen again, was the Saviour who could save them from sin.

That their testimony was effective is seen by the fact that thousands were saved and brought into the fold of Christ. Their testimony went out in power and unction of the Holy Spirit.

Look at the Apostle Peter. Imbued with the challenge from Christ, he preached the Word in power at Pentecost, with what result? Three thousand souls in one day.

Continuing steadfast in the doctrines of the apostles and in fellowship together, the church zealously proclaimed personal salvation and the Word says "the Lord added to the church daily, such as should be saved."

The First Century Church took the commission literally and before forty years had elapsed, the gospel of Christ had been preached throughout the known world, from one end of the Roman Empire to the other. And mind you, the group who took that message from the first day numbered only 120 persons.

The church made more progress toward the evangelization of the world in the first 100 years than it has in the last 1900. Why? You know the answer. Read the Book of Acts, and then look at your own attitude toward the Gospel and Christ's commission to "Go ye" and you can answer the question for yourself.

Brethren, what about this challenge–are we going to let "His Testimony" fail by not giving urgent heed to His commission?

I don't believe that you will fail Him. He said "Go ye" and I believe every last one of you are going to put your heart and mind and body to the great task of making known to a world lost in sin, that Christ Jesus is the need of their lives.

Somehow these words seem to ring through my heart, and they truly are the promise of the Lord:

"Behold I have set before thee an open door, and no man can shut it; for thou hast a little strength; and hast kept my word, and hast not denied my name.

"Behold I will make them of the synagogue of Satan, which say they are Jews, and are not, but do lie; behold, I will make them to come and worship before thy feet, and to know that I have loved thee.

"Because thou hast kept the word of my patience, I also will keep thee from the hour of temptation, which shall come upon all the world, to try them that dwell upon the earth.

"Behold, I come quickly; hold that fast which thou hast, that no man take thy crown." (Revelation 3:8-11)

CHAPTER IV

"...it is required in stewards that a man be found faithful."
1 Corinthians 4:2

Ten years have passed since first the Lord began to bless. "Great is Thy Faithfulness" is the song we must sing to the Lord. But what about my responsibility to Him? God has said in His Word that as a minister of His Word, I have a responsibility. Indeed, I am constantly aware that I am held accountable to Him for the care of many souls.

This is a sobering truth from God's Word. Every believer is saved and secure in Christ. He is in the family of God and has eternal life. A truth, though, that must never be overlooked is that we believers must all appear before the judgement seat of Christ to give an account for the deeds done in the body. It is on the basis of that reckoning that we are rewarded or fail of reward. Because I want a "well done thou good and faithful servant," my desire is to be found faithful to God for my stewardship.

We tender therefore an account of our ministry. In "His Testimony," seven ways were presented in which this testimony was peculiar to the Lord. These seven things evidenced a position of faithfulness to the Lord and His Word. I come back to these seven for a check-up today.

Then, we were sure that the great ministry of our church was magnifying the Holy Bible as the Word of Life, inspired of God, and given to us for doctrine and direction. In those days we affirmed our belief in the verbal and plenary inspiration of the Bible. Ten years have passed and our belief has never wavered. It is still the "Old Book and the Old Faith," the rock on which we stand.

Ten years ago, we were sure that the great three-fold

ministry of Christ was found in His death, His resurrection and His coming again. His precious sacrifice for sins at Calvary was mighty in our ministry. His resurrection life and glory was our living hope. His pre-millennial and personal return was "that blessed hope" of His church. To these great truths we have held unfailingly during the years. For nine years now we have been privileged to conduct the Immanuel Church on the Air on radio station WMBG, and every week the listening audience hears these closing words from our lips, "We preach Christ, crucified, risen, coming again."

Ten years ago, we believed that salvation was through the work of Christ, and in Him alone. We believed then that God could save men through simple childlike faith in the crucified and risen Lord. Today, we still believe it and witness the salvation of souls in the same old way.

Ten years ago, we believed in the person and work of the Holy Spirit, as a vital factor in the life and work of the believer. We still believe it and have lived to see the Spirit of God work marvels before our eyes.

Ten years ago, we believed and taught that there must be a demand for consecration and separation on the part of the believer. That a clean, separated church, taking its stand against the world and worldliness was essential to God's will, we have consistently preached. We haven't moved an inch from that place, and that stand we have been forced to take even to losing friends. But our stand we have taken there, and God helping us, we will have no other.

Ten years ago, we had faith in God to supply all needs, and we held then that extraneous money raising plans were not God's way, but that there was a Bible way, and that way we should follow. Not a single supper, social, sale, or any other device has been used to raise money here. These unscriptural plans were cut loose the first week of our ministry and we have never needed to go back to them. God has proven Himself sufficient to these things. We still stand there, too.

Back ten years ago, we believed and still believe now that the great commission "Go ye" is the commission to the church today. We have seen God's blessing on this, too. What a fat cry the $274.00 for missions that first year is, from the $8,301.58 for the six months closing May 30, 1944. As an everlasting testimony to what God can do with a church that really gets down to business with God on this matter of missions, we give you a comparative statement of giving to missions over a period of nearly ten years:

For the year 1934	$ 274.00
For the year 1935	(Record missing)
For the year 1936	566.19
For the year 1937	926.46
For the year 1938	1,356.30
For the year 1939	1,292.43
For the year 1940	1,347.47
For Eleven Months to Nov. 30, 1941	3,290.01
For Year ending Nov. 30, 1942	7,311.57
For Year ending Nov. 30, 1943	14,500.00
For Six Months ending May 30, 1944	8,301.58

When we have our semi-annual Rally in November, 1944, we hope to see the total reach onward toward $20,00.00 for the current year.

It is not required in a steward that he be found popular. Nor is it required of him that he be successful. It is, however, required that he be found possessed of that characteristic called "faithfulness". We make this report of our stewardship to the Lord to await His judgement of our faithfulness. We publish this report to the people of God and to the world, as a testimony to the glory of our God and our Christ.

****

A man, who was saved eight years ago here, states as his testimony: "I was saved May, 1936. The Lord has done many things for me. Cured me of tobacco and drink habits, also many other things I was doing for pleasure. Now they are a displeasure and I thank God I am saved and on my way to heaven."

A twenty-year-old mother writes this touching testimony: "Being saved when I started to Immanuel, but not fully consecrated, I was worldly. After hearing the Word faithfully taught, I gave Christ all and am happy in His service."

From a young mother this word of testimony comes: "I want to praise the Lord for saving me three years ago. I know "He is able to keep that which I have committed unto Him against that day."

From a nineteen-year-old girl, this testimony speaks: "August, 1943, I came here (Richmond) to live. I found a gospel church to attend, and I truly do praise the Lord for Immanuel Church and the many spiritual blessings I have received there."

A devoted Christian and worker in the Sunday School writes: "I have been lead to a deeper understanding of God's Word, and I praise Him for the wonderful spiritual growth in our church in the last ten years. God answers prayer."

CHAPTER V

"The Lord gave the Word; great was the company of those that published it." Psalm 68:11

God uses human instruments to accomplish His purpose. Because this is true, then it is but right that we give one chapter of this little book to pay fitting tribute to such as have been used of the Lord to make this work possible. This is in no sense a magnifying of the flesh. We must always remember that the Word is God's, and that He gave it. There is no sin in remembering "the company of those that published it."

First of all, surely this ministry would have been greatly handicapped had it not been for the devotion, the sacrifice and the humble support of the one the Lord gave me as my helpmate. God alone knows the trials and the struggles of a Pastor's wife. I give thanks to the Lord for providing me with one who has been a blessing to me and my work.

Then, there are the fine men and women God has put around us. Sturdy and sane deacons were His gift to us for many battles with Satan. Teachers He gave us and workers who could explain the truth of the Word.

Ungrateful indeed would we be if we failed to remember that God has given us members and friends of this work whose faithful praying and support have been used of God to carry on. There are those who have been led forth by the Lord to go out into paths unusual. Some have given of their best to preaching and testifying in jails, in hospitals, in the City Home. Others have gone into the public parks to give forth their testimony. Still others have sought for places of testimony in neglected areas, like the colored folk's mission in Woodville. Others have found a place of testimony teaching the Child Evangelism classes on week days, and some are finding a blessing in the Miracle Book club work.

Some of our folk have found fields of service in places that require even more of their time, so that one of our young men, with his wife, now ministers to a field of flourishing churches in Eastern Virginia. Another of our young men is just now beginning a new pastorate in Pennsylvania, and his good wife will continue to be a great help to him there. Another young couple have just taken up their work in a field of three churches down in North Carolina, where the Lord will surely use them in His service. From "way down in the deep South comes word of successful evangelistic campaigns being conducted by two more of our young men who are teamed up with their families for full time evangelistic work. Here at home one of our young ladies gives her full time as a local Child Evangelism Fellowship worker, reaching out into the lives of hundreds of children. And then there is that young deacon who is launching out on a most unusual ministry that may eventually send him out into full time service. As he preaches every morning on the radio, and almost every Sunday somewhere, God uses him to win souls. Then there is that deacon, a successful business man, who finds time to go out week after week to preach the Word in missions, churches or wherever God opens doors.

These form the company of those who publish this Word. And still there are more, for what about the eight young people now at Moody Bible Institute studying for definite Christian service? One of these already has been accepted as a missionary to Africa. Another has been thinking and praying about South America. Others of these are praying for the Lord's leading. At Wheaton College are two of our fine young folk preparing, and two more planning to go to prepare definitely for Christian service in the next six months; another plans to go to Moody in the fall.

Thus goes on the endless chain of those who form the company sent to publish the Word. And could we forget the evangelists the Lord has sent to us? We dare not name them for fear it would magnify men, but eleven evangelistic meetings have been spread over the years, and many souls have come to Christ. Can we ever forget the grand campaign of the Spring of 1936, when God gave us many souls in the first real campaign held after our ministry started? Surely none of us will forget the grand Mosque meeting of the Winter of 1941. What a glorious privilege it was to be one who was used of the Lord to deal with souls in the inquiry room during those six weeks. Over seven hundred souls were dealt with and many of them are staunch believers today. What boundless blessings have come to us as one after another of God's choice evangelists have come and preached the Word, and how our hearts have rejoiced as many have come to a saving knowledge of our Lord Jesus Christ! Different, indeed, were these men of God. Different in personality, different in way of presentation, different in so many ways, but all preaching the unsearchable riches of Christ. They all preached Christ as Saviour and Lord. God blessed them to us.

Another ministry we have not neglected is that of building up these converts in the faith. We have sought through Bible teaching and preaching to do our best with the 'corn bread preachin' we do. God has also sent to us many fine Bible teachers to back up the truth we were so crudely giving forth, men who could teach about deeper life, doctrine, devotional subjects, prophecy and the like. Some of these visiting brethren took us into word studies, some followed doctrinal themes, some would take us through a book of the Bible such as Romans, I John, Jude or Ephesians. They all ministered the Word to us so we understood it better after they left, and we felt we were drawn closer to the Lord.

Then there were the missionaries who came to turn our eyes and hearts to a world vision. God was good to send to us several men who were choice spirits and well informed as leaders of faith mission boards. They helped us much in shaping the policy and program of our missionary endeavor. And what shall we say about the countless multitude of missionaries who from time to time have been our way? Every one left a blessing. Here was one from China and there one from Africa. They came from South America, Central America and the West Indies. They came from the mountain areas and from back woods areas where they have laboured. They are missionaries to every land, and they came our way to tell us what God was doing to win the heathen for Himself, and they pled with us to help by prayer and support to give the Word diligently. They were Ambassadors of a God giving vision to us.

All of this and much more could be said about the "company of those who published it." No one can say that any one man deserves the credit for this great work, but that the company that helped through these ten years to spread the Word includes not only the Pastor and his people, but all of these evangelists, Bible teachers, mission leaders and workers. Truly we can say without hesitation, "God gave the Word; great was the company of those that published it."

****

Another lady, a mother and teacher in the Sunday School, writes her testimony thus: "I praise the Lord for leading me to Immanuel Church. There I learned the truth of God's Word. Two years ago I rededicated my life to the Lord and now have that peace and joy that comes only in the life yielded in Christ."

Chapter VI

"Sanctify yourselves; for tomorrow the Lord will do wonders among you." Joshua 3:5

The story has been told. Ten years have passed. It seems as only yesterday that it began. How time flies! Isn't it true that what is done for the Lord must be done quickly, for time moves on so rapidly? When we review a period of time and see how fast it passed, doesn't it bring home in a real way why the Lord says, "Today if you will harden not your heart," and "Behold, today is the day of salvation" ?

And yet, there is tomorrow. There is the future. There is the onward look. There is, especially in the life of the believer in Christ, that light that shines on toward the perfect day. There is indeed the challenge to turn from that which is behind, and to press on to the goal of the high calling of God in Christ Jesus. We can't go back, we can only review. Time marches on. We must move onward in step with the fleeting hours.

What about tomorrow? We face it now, even as Joshua and the children of Israel faced it as they stood at the bank of the River Jordan. Are we now at the "Jordan River" time in the life of our church? Is there a land of promise, flowing with milk and honey ahead of us? Is there a Canaan to be conquered? In a real way, I feel that at the occasion of this tenth anniversary of our ministry at Immanuel Baptist Church, we stand ready to respond to the command of the Lord to "arise, (and) go over this Jordan, thou and all this people, unto the land which I do give to them."

As God said to Joshua, and through Joshua to the children of Israel–He speaks even to us today: "Have not I commanded thee? Be strong and of good courage; be not afraid, neither be thou dismayed; for the Lord thy God is with thee whithersoever thou goest." Today, the challenge is before us. Shall we possess the land or turn back from our great opportunity? There is but one answer, and that is, "Move forward."

But that is more easily said than done. To go forward is a challenge that must not be lightly taken. For Joshua and Israel to move forward meant at the very beginning to face the barrier of the Jordan River in the season when it was flooded and over its banks. Learn, dear ones, that whenever a challenge is given to us by the Lord, there is a barrier that must be met and passed.

I lay before you a challenge today. God's challenge it is, for I have talked with the Lord about these things and they are all a part of the great challenge of the Lord to us.

The greatest challenge to the church of God today is contained in the great commission, "Go ye therefore, and teach all nations, baptizing them in the name of the Father, and of the Son, and of the Holy Ghost; teaching them to observe all things whatsoever I have commanded you and, lo, I am with you alway, even unto the end of the world." (Matthew 28:19-20) Our challenge is to sound out the Word to the uttermost parts of the world.

More specifically, our challenge is to a greater missionary program than ever before. During the past ten years, we have been richly blessed of the Lord in this missionary work, but the future lies ahead. We have not yet reached the peak. These young folk of our church who are at school studying for definite Christian service will be going forth to fields of labor. Shortly, they will be looking across the Atlantic to the heart of Africa. God will turn faces of some to the call of China's millions. South America, the dark continent of the Western Hemisphere, will soon plead and tug at the heart strings of some of our young men and women. That will be the challenge that will come to our young folk. What shall we say to them and to God, when we face the great challenge "Go ye," and they are ready to go? Will we say, "We haven't the money to send you"? Not if we are true to the Lord, we won't. We will answer the challenge and say, "You go, son. You go, daughter. Give the best of your life to lost mankind and to the service of the Lord. We will give and give and give until the Lord comes. We will pray for you, and we will hold the fort here, while you go out there into the night and rescue souls, lost and dying in sin." Surely that is the way we will answer the challenge to this great missionary program. Fifteen thousand, eight hundred dollars last year, but never again will our missionary giving fall as low as that if we catch the vision the Lord has for us.

    I have the conviction, and it is not just a dream, that the future life of this church is bound up in this great missionary program. More important than getting new members or building new edifices, is sending out the Word. I do not mean that we shall not need a larger building to house our Bible School. By the grace of God, I am sure that is a part of the new ten years' work--if the Lord tarry. I do not mean that we not grow in numbers. By God's leading, I am sure there will come into our fellowship many precious souls and that the Lord will add such as He saves. But what I am saying is that the all-important challenge to our church is getting the Word of Life out to the corners of the earth. That is the great commission, and that is our challenge. We will not stop.

    If in the providence of the Lord, we remain to be the under-shepherd of this flock another ten years, it will be constantly over and over again, "Go ye." It will be passionately pled from a heart to whom God has spoken in such a way that it cannot but bleed for the lost heathen world. Over and over again you will hear it. "Missions." "The heathen are lost." "Men are dying in their sins." "Africans are falling by millions into Christless graves." "South America's savage Indians are lost without Christ." "China's millions long for the truth, and we must give it to them." "Christ died for the Latin Americans, and woe is me if I fail to get it to them." "Thousands of boys and girls right here in America haven't had the opportunity to hear of Christ. Come, let's give them the Gospel." That's what you are going to hear, friends.

God has burned that into my soul like a fire and it cannot be quenched. That is our great challenge today. That involves the preparation of young folk for the mission field. That involves many decisions. That involves parents who must say to sons and daughters, "Sons, daughters, go on. Leave home. Go to Moody Bible Institute. Go to Wheaton College. Go to Bob Jones College. Go to Philadelphia School of the Bible. Go to Columbia Bible College. Go, even though it breaks up our little family. You go. Then go on to Africa, and to China, and to Latin America and to India, and the islands of the sea. You go, and if we never see you here on earth again, we'll have a happy meeting when we meet the Lord in the air." Then we will rejoice that we gave our lives together to win souls from every tribe and nation. Then we shall rejoice together with the Lord for eternity. Oh, that's what I mean. That's our challenge. Shall we meet it and go through with it to God's glory?

Joshua and the children of Israel heard the challenge of the Lord. Their challenge was to take Canaan. Our challenge is to take Christ to a lost and dying world. How were they to prepare for that conquest? God said, "Sanctify yourselves." Now that is a peculiar thing to say, yet it is the word of God. What did God mean when He said, "Sanctify yourselves?" What does it mean to sanctify one's self?

First, to sanctify means to set apart. The work of sanctification is the work of God. It is true that a believer who is saved is sanctified, because to be saved means to be set apart. But in this text it is said that God told the Israelites to sanctify themselves. What could that mean? Well, God sanctifies people, sets them apart to His own purposes. But there is a further truth to learn, and that is that the person God sets apart to a certain purpose, must surrender himself to that purpose. It does not mean that we make ourselves holy, but that we make ourselves wholly His. God has set every believer apart to His purpose; it remains for every believer to set himself apart to that same purpose. When God makes known His will in a life, it remains for that one to surrender to God's will and purpose. When that is done the two, God and the believer, are one in the task. When that is true, no man or power in heaven or earth can thwart the working out of the plan of God. Had you ever envisioned what a church of five hundred members might do if every one of them, aware that God had sanctified them to his purpose, in turn sanctified themselves fully to that purpose? I challenge you to make that surrender right now. I dare you to lay this booklet aside and get on your knees before the Lord and actually surrender your whole life and will to Him.

But sanctifying means more than surrendering. It means cleansing. The children of Israel knew no form of sanctification that did not include washings. Washing was for cleanliness. God wants clean vessels for His service. God does not work with dirty tools. He will not use unclean vessels to pour forth the water of life. If the church was ever in need of clean, forthright, upright, uncontaminated Christian character, it is today. Some one said, "Character is like a fence; no amount of whitewashing will straighten it up." Character is something God puts into Christians, and it must be kept straight and clean. To sanctify one's self means to cleanse. As I prepare this message my Bible lies open before me and the verse that stares out at me is II Corinthians 7:11: "Having therefore these promises, dearly beloved, let us cleanse ourselves from all filthiness of the flesh and spirit, perfecting holiness in the fear of God." That's what it means to sanctify yourselves.

Oh, what God can do with a man or a woman who is surrendered and clean! That is the challenge I give you today. "Go across the Jordan and possess the land," God is saying to us, but only those who are fully surrendered and clean can be greatly used in this task.

Out of my heart I want to talk to our young folk. Listen, young folk, many of you in the last few years have responded to altar calls to say that you wanted to dedicate your lives to Christian service. On one occasion I saw over one hundred of you come down to the altar for that purpose. You were in earnest, I know. I believe in you, young folk. I believe you are honest, and I believe you are in earnest. But listen, all of you haven't gotten into the will of God for your lives. I'm talking to you earnestly now, and out of my heart. What's the matter? What has held you back from getting down to business with the Lord? May it be a good idea right here and now to get down to business with the Lord? Have you let something of the world spoil your clean hands and hearts? Oh, God wants you. He wants your life. He wants to bless you. He wants to use you. But God can't use you to the full until you are His to the full. Surrender your life in full to Him. Come to Him in confession of sin, and cleanse the soiled spots, that you may be a clean vessel for the Master's use. It is essential, if we truly sanctify our lives to Him, that we be surrendered and that we be clean.

And one thing more. To sanctify ourselves means to separate ourselves. Now here is a place where we have a hard time with ourselves, because talking separation is different from practicing it. Separation has a two-fold aspect. There is separation from, and there is separation unto. In the 6th chapter of II Corinthians we are told not to fellowship together with unrighteousness. We are told not to commune with those who are of darkness. We are not to accord with the things of Belial. We are warned against partaking with infidelity. We are told not to be in agreement with anything that is against the temple of God. If one wants to know what and whom to separate from, here is his answer. Whatever is of unbelief or lack of trust in Christ, do not yoke up with that. Whatever is in fellowship with that which is not righteous, do not fellowship with that. Whatever is in communion with the darkness of sin, do not commune with that. Whatever is in accord with Belial (Satan), that which is sinful, do not accord with that. Whatever is a partaking together with that which is not faithfulness to Christ, do not partake of that. Whatever is in agreement with idolatry (and that is disagreement with that which is consistent in the temple of God,) that is the thing with which you are not to agree. A real heart-searching in these verses will give you a real idea of what real separation is.

But we are not only to be separated from, we are to be separated unto. Separation from, means to part with; separation unto, means to partake with. Separation from, means not yielding to sin; separation unto means yielding all to God. We are to separate from the sins of this world; we are to separate unto the Saviour as Lord in this world. To separate from the world and its lusts means to leave all that was our former love; while to separate unto Christ and the things of the Lord means to lose all things in our present Lover. Oh, to fall in love anew with the Lord Jesus. To be separated from, is to break conformity with this world; and to be separated unto, means to be transformed by the will of God. (Romans 12:1-2)

This is what we must do, friends. We must sanctify

ourselves. We must surrender anew, we must cleanse anew, we must separate anew. That's what it means to sanctify ourselves. Why? Well, let's go back to our text: "For tomorrow the Lord..." Today *we* sanctify, tomorrow the *Lord* ...*In the Lord* is where our dependence should be found. And may I call your attention to the fact that the word "LORD" here is the word "Jehovah"? The name is that ascribed to God in His redemptive relationship. It is the Lord Jehovah who yesterday redeemed Israel, who is talking. It is Jehovah who through blood redeemed the Israelites. It is Jehovah who met the adversary of that nation, even Pharaoh, and successfully wrought to bring these people out of bondage with a mighty hand. It was the same Jehovah, who when these poor people knew not the way, who opened the Red Sea and led them through on dry land, forever to be freed from the bondage of the Egyptians. It was this same Jehovah who fed them with manna from Heaven. It was the same Jehovah who gave them the water from the rock. Yes, it was the same Jehovah who had brought them all the way to the land of promise. And now he is saying "Sanctify yourselves, for tomorrow Jehovah."

    Now this Jehovah of the Old Testament is the redemptive name of God for that time, but the redemptive name of God today is Jesus. What the name "Jehovah" meant in those days to Israel in national deliverance, the name of the Lord Jesus means to the believer today is his personal redemption from sin. Sin today holds the sinner in bondage, even as Pharaoh held the nation Israel in national bondage. Today, it is through the power of the shed blood of the Lord Jesus that men are redeemed from sin's bondage. Then, it was the blood on the door post that guaranteed deliverance from slavery in Egypt. As the children of Israel were delivered then from that bondage through the power of Jehovah, the believer is delivered now from the power of sin's bondage by the power of the eternal Son, Jesus Christ. But that is not all. The Lord Jehovah, who brought them out of Egypt, will lead them into Canaan. The same Lord Jesus, who redeemed us out of sin's bondage will lead us unto the blessed land of our spiritual Canaan. Yesterday, Jehovah led them out–tomorrow the same Jehovah leads them in. What a precious truth there is here. The Lord does not save us and drop us, but He saves us and leads us on ... "for tomorrow the Lord." Yes, it is true that as He was with us during the days that have gone on, He will go before us as we go on into the years ahead. In the challenge He gives us here, do not overlook that when He challenges us to move forward, He goes on before us. Tomorrow, when we find ourselves in a war of conquest for souls of men, the Lord Jesus will have gone on before us. The Captain of our salvation is not an officer who pushes his men into the battle and stays behind to drive them on. He is a real Captain and He leads on. We can sing it truthfully:

Onward Christian soldiers, marching as to war,
With the Cross of Jesus going on before.

"Tomorrow the Lord will do." Look at this sentence again. It is the heart of a great challenge, but the Lord looms before us in every turn. The Lord is not asking us to do, but the challenge is that *He* will do. It seems almost a paradox, that the children of Israel were told to take the land, and then He says, "The *Lord* will do." How true it is though, God challenges us to make ourselves ready. The challenge to us is to sanctify ourselves; to surrender, to cleanse, to separate. Then God says *He* will do. It is not true that what the Lord plans to do is through sanctified vessels? Indeed it is, but it is to be His doing.

Friends, Christian friends, brethren of the fellowship of the Lord, hear me this day. It was the Lord who redeemed us, and it is the Lord who leads on, and it is the Lord who will possess the land and conquer it. We shall not do it. There is, however, a precious truth for us to lay hold of here. While God is going to do it, we as the humble tools in His hand must be surrendered, clean and separated, so the end can be accomplished through us. To walk across the Jordan River on dry land did not require the building of dams and water barriers, because when the feet of those people touched the waters they parted, flood or no flood. "Tomorrow the Lord will do." The parting of the Jordan waters was His doing, not theirs. Tomorrow we shall start to possess the land, and as we start into the conquest we shall reach a flooded Jordan that no human could manage to cross in his own strength and power. So tomorrow we must depend on the Lord, and "tomorrow the Lord will do." What was required of the people? Only this–"Sanctify yourselves." It appears to be true, that the power of God works on behalf of the surrendered, clean, separated people of His choosing. They walked on dry land by the power of God that day, but only sanctified people could walk through dry shod.

      To see the walls of Jericho fall did not require battering rams and artillery fire and fierce charging infantrymen. That would be the human way to conquer. No, that was not the way of the Lord. "Sanctify yourselves," that was what the people did, and an evidence of their surrender, cleansing and separation, was their walk, and though it may look foolish to tramp around the city every day, and seven times on the seventh day, what they did was evidence that they were sanctified to the will of God. But did they fight to take the city? No. "Tomorrow the Lord will do," and through His power and His alone the walls of Jericho came in a heap to the ground. A sanctified people and a God who could do marvels! It seems that it is true that God delights to exercise His power in behalf of the people who have sanctified themselves, who have surrendered, cleansed and separated themselves wholly to Him. That is what God wants of you and me. Tomorrow the *Lord* will do, " and for *you* and for *me* it is, "Sanctify yourselves."

And what will the Lord do? Listen: "The Lord will do wonders among you." God is a great God who is capable of doing wonders. Do you believe that? He worked wonders in Israel. He can work wonders here. Dear friends, do not underestimate God's ability in our midst. The problem of how God can work wonders among us in the years that are to come, is not a matter of whether God can or not. God can. The problem is whether we are willing to "sanctify ourselves."

Perhaps no man has been more used of the Lord in the past hundred years than Dwight L. Moody. His name is a monument to Christian faith. You can hardly go into a hamlet of our country and not find someone who knows about D. L. Moody. Once, while on a trip to Great Britain, Moody heard a man say something that caught his attention. That man said: "The world has yet to see what God will do with and for and through and in and by the man who is fully and wholly consecrated to Him." D. L. Moody heard that statement and meditated it in his mind. "He said 'a man'", thought Moody; "not a great man, nor a learned man, nor a rich man, nor a wise man, nor an eloquent man, nor a smart man, but simply 'a man'. I am a man, and it lies with the man himself whether he will or will not make that entire and full consecration. I will try my uttermost to be that man." That decision made that day by D. L. Moody is the thing that text challenges us to do. D. L. Moody's life was an eloquent testimony that God can "do wonders," if we but respond to what God asks of us. The challenge stands: "Sanctify yourselves." The promise of the Lord is certain to follow: "For tomorrow the Lord will do wonders among you."

****

**Editor's note: "GOD DID IT" is reprinted by permission and is complete as originally written and published in 1944.